THE AUTHENTIC LEADER AS SERVANT (ALS)

**ALS II COURSE 3
EMPATHY LEADERSHIP
Attributes, Principles, and Practices**

SYLVANUS N. WOSU, Ph.D

THE AUTHENTIC LEADER AS SERVANT
ALS II COURSE 3
Developing Empathy Leadership Attributes, Principles, and Practices

© Copyright 2024 by Sylvanus N. Wosu Ph.D.

Printed in the United States of America
ISBN: 978-1-960224-52-1

All rights reserved. No part of this book may be reproduced or transmitted in any form or by any means, electronic or mechanical, including photocopying, recording, or by any information storage and retrieval system, without permission in writing from the copyright owner.

Bible quotations are from the New King James (NKJV) version of the Bible unless otherwise indicated.

Other versions used in this book are the New International Version (NIV), New Living Translation (NLT), King James Version (KJV), English Standard Version (ESV), and Good News Translation (GNT). Unless otherwise specified, NKJV should be assumed.

The views expressed in this work are solely those of the author and do not necessarily reflect the views of the publisher, and the publisher disclaims any responsibility for them.

To order additional copies of this book, contact:
Proisle Publishing Services LLC
39-67 58th Street, 1st floor
Woodside, NY 11377, USA
Phone: (+1 646-480-0129)
info@proislepublishing.com

TABLE OF CONTENTS

FOREWORD	XI
ACKNOWLEDGMENTS	XV
DEDICATION	XVII
PREFACE	19

- About Leader As Servant Leadership (LSL) Model --------------------------- 22
- About the Authentic Leader as Servant (ALS) ---------------------------------- 25
- About the ALS Courses -- 26

CHAPTER 1
UNDERSTANDING LEADERSHIP ATTRIBUTES   35

- Functional Definitions --- 35
- Comparisons With Other Works -- 40
- Principle of Leadership Attribute -- 42
- Authentic Leadership Attributes --- 43
- Summary 1 Understanding Leadership Process -------------------------------- 48

CHAPTER 2
EMPATHY LEADERSHIP ATTRIBUTE   51

- Servant Leadership Empathy Attribute --- 52
- Principle of Leadership Empathy Attribute-------------------------------------- 54
- Summary 2 Empathy Leadership Attribute -------------------------------------- 56

CHAPTER 3
DEVELOPING EMPATHY– SELF AWARENESS ATTRIBUTE   59

- Biblical Examples of Self-awareness -- 59
- Develop a Desire for Self-assessments --- 62
- Develop an Inner Perception of Personality ------------------------------------ 63
- Develop a Sense of External Perceptions-- 65
- Develop Yourself from Experiential Learning---------------------------------- 67
- Summary 3 Developing Empathy–Self Awareness ---------------------------- 70

CHAPTER 4
DEVELOPING EMPATHY–SYMPATHY   73

- Understand emotions in communication -- 74
- Summary 4 Developing Empathy–Sympathy------------------------------------ 74

CHAPTER 5
DEVELOPING EMOTIONAL SELF-REGULATION   77
Summary 5 Developing Emotional Self-Regulation ---- 79

CHAPTER 6
DEVELOPING EMPATHY–COMPASSION   81
Develop a heart of humility ---- 82
Empathy-compassion is sharing and caring ---- 83
Emulate the Empathy of God ---- 84
A Case of Complete Empathy ---- 86
Self-Centeredness Paralyzes Compassion ---- 88
A Case of Sharing Self in Empathy ---- 90
Summary 6 Developing Empathy–Compassion ---- 92

TOPIC INDEX   95
REFERENCES   97

FOREWORD

The modern world today is obsessed with standardization and modalities. As a result, in the realm of leadership, many books have spout associated leadership theories and models and explain them as the path to follow. However, the critical dimensions that distinguish the effectiveness of any leadership process are the values and attribute the leader brings to the table; desired change is influenced by leadership styles or standards. These many standards and theories of leadership often are not in step with the changing times or the followers' needs. The trend is a bit like stocking different kinds of foods in a grocery store and expecting that they will meet everybody's needs the same way and at all times. Aisles are packed with varieties of food with expiration dates in the future, but getting the best deal on the products is what really matters to those who buy and use the products

In many ways, this is the state of leadership in the modern world. Increasingly, even leaders of public institutions are tasked with turning a profit for themselves or the organization they serve. The idea of a "leader" seems to float uneasily alongside the ranks of fundraisers or profit raisers in contrast to any kind of role model for followers or employees. That which is knowable, measurable, and marketable has surpassed the difficult intangibility of strong moral leadership attributes as the central guideline for achievement and success.

In this complicated space, Dr. Sylvanus Wosu introduces his complex idea of the Leader as a Servant Leadership, which is in this book, modeled on Christian tradition. Like all intricate ideas, Dr. Wosu's central point depends on a paradox: a person is best qualified to lead when he or she is most ready to serve. This paradox has been monopolized rhetorically by "public servants" who often serve either self-interest or the interests of specific lobbies. The Authentic Leader as Servant penetrates past the superficial concept of "serving" and details the internal state of true servitude or Servanthood.

While the book is primarily focused on the Christian model of leadership attributes such as discipleship, empathy, affection, and Servanthood, it does so not merely on the grounds of blind faith, but rather via numerous contemporary sociological and business-driven studies on how leaders should seek a leader-follower relationship that is simultaneously productive and nurturing. Dr. Wosu's most piercing insights always involve this secular–Christian dialogue. This book demonstrates that Christ's model for leadership is one that may exist successfully outside the confines of a faith relationship; it places the values of Christ's religious significance in leadership at the center of the framework. It is clear from Dr. Wosu's generous own life story of faith—a faith tested by humbling difficulties—is at the center of both his orientation and motivation for writing.

In language that is so concise, it is often illustrated in mathematical formulas; Dr. Wosu explains the deep structural integrity of Christ's Leader as the Servant Leadership model. One could imagine leaders of any doctrine benefiting from the analyses contained in these pages. The book's message repeatedly encourages the reader to imagine a scenario or reflect on memories and personal experiences to prove or test its many points. Thus, the book depends on a form of praxis, a lesson that could be or has been enacted, by the participating reader. I am very impressed at the volume and level of thinking of the author. Parts of the book involve his personal story, which is especially riveting. I cannot imagine what he had to endure, which he referred to as a" wilderness walk," to accomplish the goal he set for himself. His life stories on these pages are inspiring and stimulating.

In this way, the text eschews dogmatism in favor of the self-discovery Socratic Method of teaching and learning. The reader is not badgered into complying with a religious objective but is rather asked to consider the applicability of difficult biblical concepts in relation to modern life. It is a fascinating and very thought-provoking read.

Hence, the book does not seek to make the leader a servant, a cookie-cutter corporate buzzword, but rather asks the reader to imagine him or herself interacting with a range of concepts. One of Dr. Wosu's great strengths is his reservation when it comes to forcing his reading's interpretation on the material he presents.

The book parallels Biblical and modern leadership scenarios in ways that consistently provoke thought, and while it is clear Dr. Wosu has his particular leadership style; the space for the reader's own thoughts is always left open.

The book could not have been written in any other way with integrity. Its format and formulas are offered to the reader of the leader as a servant role that it analyzes in its pages. To find a text that instructs from this humble position is profoundly refreshing in a genre that is often packaged inside a cover with a sizeable picture of the "modest" author, smiling egotistically beneath a name spelled out in large, gold lettering. Throughout its pages, this text feels as if it serves the reader.

In the end, this is the most satisfying aspect of the book. There is no standardized approach to achieving successful leadership. There is no promise of power and a bigger payday; in fact, the book often proffers just the opposite. The reader is not encouraged to devalue the experience of leadership by finding some economic metric for marking success but is rather asked to think deeply about the most basic elements of internal and social interaction within the framework of a Christian tradition. What this means will be different for every reader. Indeed, even in the context of single chapters, I found myself questioning or re-evaluating moments of my own life. This book serves; it doesn't feel like filling in multiple-choice questions, staring at a wall of flavorless grocery products, or hearing the endless servant promises of today's political scene. It feels like a humble invitation to consider a single paradoxical element of a profoundly productive tradition.

-Tobias Bates

ACKNOWLEDGMENTS

A book on leadership attributes as aspects of Servant Leadership sprouted from the wealth of knowledge and the inspirations of many other leaders. Their writings were sources of inspiration, challenges, and examples of excellence to emulate. I acknowledge the leaders listed below for their help in one way or the other. I am very grateful and I hereby express my appreciation and thanks:

Mr. Wayne Holt, introduced me first to the subject of Servanthood in one of our Stephen Ministerial Training classes, and he is the one who has conducted his life as a leader–servant; he encouraged me throughout my writing;

Dr. Harvey Borovetz, Distinguished Professor and Chair of the Bioengineering Department, is a leader-servant in many ways, he modeled Servanthood and encouragement attributes throughout his leadership in an academic setting.

Dr. Clifford and Dr. Patience Obih, in so many measures exemplified the practical leadership attributes discussed in this book.

Pastor Lance Lecocq, Lead Pastor of Monroeville Assembly of God, for his excellent model of servanthood, empowerment, and emulation attributes to the ministerial team, I am thankful for his motivation and encouragement throughout the several hours on this project;

To my administrative assistant, Ms. Terri Cook, who was always the first to review the manuscript; I am very grateful for her dedication.

To the African Christian Fellowship USA, institutions, and all other organizations where I have served in one leadership capacity or the other, thank you for affording me senior leadership positions that provided the leadership platform and opportunities to grow as a leader.

Dr. Lawrence Owoputi, a brother I am proud to call my friend; for his dedication to serving others, his generosity, healing care, and responsibility attributes during our term in office and in chapter leadership positions; he taught me that excellent following is also part of good leadership;

To Tobias Bates, for his editorial work on the original draft of the book, and his dedication to completing the work.

Mr. Edward F. Kondis, a member of our Engineering Board of Visitors, for his always encouraging and moral support;

Dr. Enefaa N. Wosu, my wife and life partner, for her love, commitment, and prayer support, especially during those long night hours I was not there for her and her constant reminder of who I must be as a leader-servant. Without her support, forbearance, wisdom, and encouragement, this project would not have been completed; I say, thank you very much.

And to God alone be all the glory and honor for the divine inspiration and guidance in initiating and completing this life-transforming book project.

DEDICATION

I humbly submit this book back unto the gracious hands of God who inspired the writings through His Holy Spirit!

I dedicate this book to my virtuous wife of 45 years, Rev. (Dr.) Enefaa Wosu whose spiritual leadership is an important gateway to our home, and to our four wonderful children—Prof. Eliada Wosu-Griffin EL, HeCareth, Tamuno-Emi, and Chidinma. From them all, I learnt what it meant to be a leader-servant. I could not be blessed with better teachers.

PREFACE

What characteristics did Biblical leaders like the Apostle Paul, Moses, Joshua, and Nehemiah as servants of their people display outwardly that distinguished them from other leaders, both then and now? The Apostle Paul kept his focus to *emulate* Christ and endured all the infirmities and persecutions he suffered to complete his goal to preach the gospel of Jesus Christ. He inspired Timothy and others through his effective *discipleship* leadership to imitate him as he emulated Christ. Moses' outward display of his *trust* in God's power earned him a good level of trust from the people and empowered him for the mission of delivery of God's children from bondage in Egypt; he had to *reproduce* himself in Joshua to complete the mission. But the greatest of them was Jesus Christ, who humbly sacrificed His life to finish the work of redemption. In His *Servanthood*, commitment, and love for the people, He became the ultimate *model* of a leader as a servant to *emulate*.

Let's consider for a moment secular leaders in these current times! For example, think of Henry Ford, who founded the successful Ford Motor Company; Bill Gates who created the global empire that is Microsoft; Albert Einstein, who in many ways is synonymous with a genius for his contributions to modern physics; Abraham Lincoln, remembered as one of the greatest presidents and leaders of United States; and many others like these we cannot mention. What did all these leaders have in common? What propelled them to turn their initial failures or challenges into eventual successes? None had a direct mentor or inherited any fortune from their parents. Nevertheless, they all eventually succeeded. These people can be distinguished from others based on their self-will to succeed, their self-confidence and belief in themselves, their self-determination, and their perseverance, among other characteristics. The distinguishing characteristics displayed externally in service or relationships toward others are the outward functional attributes that define that leader.

Think about yourself as a student, faculty member, or that new executive. What was it that made your journey to success different and even great? Students and colleagues, when they see or hear about my display of what I have referred to as the 'wilderness walk of faith', have asked me to share the critical attitudinal elements that made me remain inwardly resilient and undaunted and yet outwardly joyful in the difficulties I had faced. This book is the result of those reflections. Let me explain one such teaching moment.

Many years ago, sitting in my research lab on a Saturday morning trying to finish writing my dissertation, a fellow graduate student walked into the room to talk with me. He was contemplating terminating his graduate studies. He was a privileged single male student but felt the load was just too much.

"Sylvanus," he asked, with seriousness in his eyes, "your research advisor suggested that I should ask you, 'what is it that makes you tick?'.'What is it about you that makes you joyful and at peace with yourself and determined to finish, no matter the situations and high expectations we face in this department?"

What he asked me were deeply reflective questions, but I was willing and excited to answer them. Even so, before I do, let's look at the context. At that period in my life, I had four little children as a graduate student; in fact, more children than any of the faculties at that time, except for one faculty member who had eight children. I received little or no support from the department. I was then an international alien, did not qualify for financial aid, and was not given any research assistant position. I was, therefore, self-supported with two off-campus part-time jobs. I joked at being a minority of minorities, the only student in the department with such a label,—but I was self-willed to succeed. My adaptability attribute, coupled with perseverance and resilience, was all that I needed to succeed despite the odds against me. In every exam, homework assignment, or project I had to compete with students with full financial aid, plus they had nothing to distract their attention from their studies. I lived with the attitude that using disadvantages as an excuse was not an option. Aspiring to earn my Ph.D. was a life dream, and I was willing to give my ultimate best to actualize that dream even in the face of challenges. The choice was mine!

So I looked at my classmate and all I could see was a student striding through a valley through which I also walked. He needed me to show him how to walk the walk, to empathize with him. To answer his question, I smiled, not that I wanted to, but because it was just who I was. The joy he attributed to me was an overflow of my appreciation of God's grace that His life in me was externally manifesting His light to bless someone else. It was a great teaching moment; I capitalized on it to tell my classmate that my joy was not about me. He could see physically but about He who was in me, he could not see in the flesh; I needed him to know that I was just showing forth His life in me. At first, my classmate did not understand the spiritual prose or metaphor I was using. He looked surprised but open to hearing more.

I did not ask if he was a Christian. However, right on my desk was my small green pocket Bible. I opened to 2 Corinthians 12:9 (NIV) and handed it to him to read. As he read the passage: "But he said to me, 'My grace is sufficient for you, for my power is made perfect in weakness.' Therefore, I will boast all the more gladly about my weaknesses, so that Christ's power may rest on me," I noticed how absorbed he was in the words

He looked astonished and read it again, this time silently. "This is interesting, but what does this mean?" He asked. I took his question to mean, "How does this relate to my question?

I explained to my friend that the external attitudes he or my advisors saw in me that warranted the question, "What makes you tick" were inspired by my inner value system based on my faith in this same Christ and His teachings. My desire to manifest His life and self-confidence is all because of what He has promised in His word if I believed. I have believed His words and have gained self-determination and faith to make the right choices through Him for my life, and his spirit has given me perseverance and resilience to focus on finishing strong in pursuit of any goal. "With that faith, I have continued, more passionately and excitedly; I can look at my challenges and vulnerabilities and delight joyfully in them, even as an alien minority of minorities! His grace and power have empowered me to do all things I want to do. That is what makes me tick," I explained.

He looked at me as if he got his answer. "Wow, thanks!" he said, looking inspired and ready to face his challenges. As we concluded with a prayer, and he stood up to leave, I pointed empathetically to his face and said, "If I made it despite my challenges, you have absolutely no excuse but to persevere to complete your studies; you can make it too!"

It is fitting to report that this encounter with my classmate transformed his will and determination to continue. Yes, he was encouraged and went on to complete his graduate studies. He emulated self-will and perseverance from the example of the most vulnerable of all students in the department.

The inner value system of a Leader-Servant is founded not only on his faith but his self-will, coupled with self-leadership; it is the greatest mentor who can turn any situation into an inconceivable success. Self-will is the primary driver for determination, resilience, and perseverance. It is what wakes you up in the morning to ask for strength to do whatever it is you are setting out to do. Based on my life walk of faith, I can state with absolute certainty that faith is the unseen assuredness that can empower you to turn your life's probable impossibilities into great and improbable possibilities.

ABOUT LEADER AS SERVANT LEADERSHIP (LSL) MODEL

Looking at the testimony above, do you know the source that energizes the characteristics you display outside and how your inner self is related to what others see outside? What distinguishes you from others is what combines to define your attributes! As a follower, can you identify the characteristics that distinguish your leaders? As an executive, how do you base your evaluation of yourself? Or how do you evaluate that brand-new manager or new youth director you want to hire? To what do you compare the individual's qualities when you look at his CV? What is the basis of your measure? Do you know if you are a substantial leader? These personal questions and much more are the subjects of this two-volume book, 'The Authentic Leader as Servant Part I: The Outward Leadership Attributes, Principles, and Practices', is written in two parts; the second part 'The Leader as Servant Leadership Model. Part II'; deals with the Inner Strength Leadership Attributes, Principles, and Practices.

When we think about today's corporate greed, deepening divide between the haves and have-not, gridlock in political systems, conflicts and wars, high divorce rates, and the rich young ruler in the Bible, it is easy to agree that all these people share a few things in common: self-centeredness, pride, lack of compassion, and greed. There is a great need in today's suffering world for leader-servants who display leadership attributes. These attributes should be oriented toward selfless service to others. Indeed, our world is increasingly drifting away from global serving reality toward the self and apathy. The most credible message or model for a possible solution to this dilemma and the answer to several complex leadership questions can be found in the foundation of the ultimate leader-servant, Jesus Christ. This book defines the Leader as Servant Leadership attribute as the combined acts of two or more distinctive functional leadership characteristics exhibited in service and relationship toward others. There is no better time than now for a book that presents comprehensive and irrevocable facts and principles regarding how to develop effective attributes of the leader-servant.

The Leader as Servant Leadership Model

My first book on this subject, The Leader as Servant Leadership Model, explains that Jesus' servant leadership model is based on the notion of a Leader as a Servant and not on a Servant as Leader. There are four distinct differences between a Servant as Leader (Servant-leader) and the Leader as Servant (leader--servant) models. It is pertinent to highlight them here to connect to this book, Authentic Leader as Servant.

A Leader as Servant is a leader first. The leader–servant as a leader does not in the line of duty go projecting or lording his or her power and authority over others but is the person to lead the process of influencing desired changes in others through his humble example of being a servant or having a serviceable attitude toward others. He or she is a serving leader, not a lording leader. He leads as a servant by putting others' needs above his own needs and rights. Jesus emphasized the word "as" meaning that the leader (the Master) chooses to serve as a servant even though he is the leader. A leader–servant emulates Jesus, who gave up all rights, and emptied and expended Himself on His followers. He empowered them to become more like Him. A leader-servant is known as a leader first but is seen as a great leader by his humble attendant heart and acts of service to others. His greatness comes from his ability to put others above himself.

Leader as Servant is a Biblical Concept. The model or image of a humble serving leader motivated Jesus' disciples to see that if their master could do this for them, they must also be able to do it for others. Jesus clearly demonstrated the process of leader-as-servant leadership. In some cases, He chose to serve by leading when He wanted to create the image or model of the leader-servant in certain acts. In other cases, He chose to lead by serving, when he showed care and empathy toward the people and led the disciples to see empathy as a leadership attribute.

Leader as Servant is an Authentic Leadership Model to follow. The Leader as the Servant leadership model intentionally positions Jesus as an original model of a leader to follow.

He was serving His disciples to demonstrate that the process of becoming a great leader was earned through humble acts of service to others; He made them understand that He was empowering them to succeed Him as leader-servants through service to others. The result was an incomparable legacy of leadership that changed their communities. The fact that Jesus relinquished his rights or shared His power did not diminish His power and influence. In fact, his influence increased at least 11 X 100%, if we ignore the one case of Judas.

The Leader as Servant Transforms Organizational Culture. The proposed LSL model seeks to transform and sustain the community or organization by instilling key leadership values or "leadership presence" among followers or an organization's members. Change is sustained when everyone in the organization takes ownership of the change. Rather than focusing on leading more followers to be great followers who conform to the organizational culture, LSL seeks to lead and empower better leaders to be distinguished leaders and community builders.

There are four distinctions, which clearly differentiate many of the existing servants as Leader-based philosophies in relation to servant leadership from my LSL model. Even in the corporate or institutional worlds, there is nothing better than Jesus on which to base Servant Leadership. There is nothing more authentic and impacting than the servant leadership modeled by the life and teachings of Jesus Christ.

The LSL model uses exploratory questions, scenarios, and graphic visualizations to excite critical thinking in ways no other book on this subject has yet attempted. Several personal testimonies of my wilderness walk of faith with God are used to connect the reader to real-life experiences of the concepts discussed. The riveting effect is that the text engages and encourages the reader to walk through the experiences presented. The aim is to inspire the reader spiritually, mentally, and professionally with this far-reaching exposition on the subject of servant leadership.

ABOUT THE AUTHENTIC LEADER AS SERVANT (ALS)

The *Authentic Leader as Servant* argues that no leadership model is as authentic, other-centered, able to build communities, and productive and service-oriented as the model of our ultimate leader-servant, Jesus Christ. No source can provide a better point of reference than that provided in the Bible. Hence, this book aims to be more than just a text on leadership; it hopes to be a personal discovery for those who aspire to develop effective leadership attributes that grow leaders as servants who ultimately develop thriving other-centered communities. This book presents a comprehensive, biblically-based study regarding how to develop these attributes and how they are applied in a servant leadership process. In this biblical context and for clarity, Servant Leadership means *Leader-as-Servant Leadership*. A *leader-servant* refers to a *leader as a servant*, which is distinct from a servant-leader or servant as leader.

Leader as Servant Leadership attributes are shaped by the Leadership's Inner Value system, which consists of character, motivation, and commitment. The *Authentic Leader as Servant* is presented as a necessary resource to complement my *The Leader as Servant Leadership (LSL) Model*. The LSL model integrates a transformative leadership framework and interactive dimensions of Servant Leadership. Leader as Servant Leadership is a process in which a leader, in his leadership position, purposefully chooses to put others' rights and needs above his positional rights and personal needs. He then serves, enables, and empowers followers for growth that builds a thriving organization. The LSL model looks at the predominant Servant Leadership concepts and shares how they compare with biblical principles on how we should lead and be led.

ABOUT THE ALS COURSES

The three books, *LSL Model* and *The Authentic Leader as Servant (*Parts I and II), together demonstrate that with today's global visions to reach people of all races and cultures, now is the time for an authentic servant's heart of service. Those visions and the leadership processes are most effective with the appropriate leadership attributes centered more on people than on the organization, principles regarding how to develop effective attributes of leader-servant.

The ALS I and II combined presented twenty leaders as servant leadership attributes. The series of ALS courses supply training guide to understand, develop, and practice the attributes in a leadership process. Each course is independent and self-contained and does not depend on completing any other course in the series of 20 courses. It is, however strongly recommended, in fact a must read, that chapters 1 and 2 in each series be covered as they lay the foundation of LSL model on which ALS is based.

ALS (Parts I & II) Course Layout

The *Authentic Leader as Servant (ALS)* leadership (parts I and II) book has been broken down into 20 courses in workbook format to achieve three goals 1) Self-discovery of the acts of developing the attribute under review in the course, 2) deeper understanding of the principles, research and biblical teaching behind the attributes, and 3) Learning the strategies for practicing the attributes.

Instruction

The set of questions following each chapter are designed to serve as a guide to discover, explore, and practice the essential ALS leadership attributes, principles, and practices in leadership process. The questions are comprehensive review based on the content of this specific chapter only.

To maximize the learning outcomes, the learner must read through this chapter and sections. Some referenced scriptures in the book are repeated in the summaries for added review if needed, even though they were discussed in the section in which they apply.

PREFACE

> The exercises that follow each chapter will help you in not only understanding your own strength and weaknesses in your acts of the attribute but will guide you in developing practical strategies you can apply in self-leadership process or helping others grow in leadership
>
> All answers to the questions are contained in the associated chapter or sections; consultation of new sources, except for the reference scriptures, is not needed. Thus, it is expected that you answer the questions after you have read the associated section or chapter of the workbook. The scripture or other references cited are only for references as they already discussed in the book

ALS II Course 1: Adaptability Leadership Attribute—*Flexibility overcomes rigidity in new and changing situations.*

Adaptability is framed as an inner strength quality of a leader in responding to changing needs or situations in a service mission. According to the Army training Handbook, adaptability is "an individual's ability to recognize changes in the environment, identify the critical elements of the new situation, and trigger changes accordingly to meet new requirements." God showed Moses adaptability when he empowered him to use the rod in his hand as an instrument for the mission ahead of him. This course will attempt to give meanings to personal reflective questions to discover the distinguishing characteristics of Leadership Adaptability. Numerous techniques, personal examples, empirical case studies, and applications of the adaptability developing strategies are discussed concepts. Practice questions at the end of each chapter are used to guide your development and to frame meanings out of the content to improve your acts of adaptability in a leadership process.

ALS II Course 2: Courage Leadership Attribute—*Courage is the inner strength of the mind to triumph over paralyzing fears of purposeful action that yields good success*

Courage Leadership Attribute is the lynchpin of effective Servant Leadership that supports the display of all the other attributes? Having the inner strength of character and convictions to persevere and hold on to new and often misunderstood ideas in the face of opposition takes courage—inner strength to triumph over the fear of failure or danger. It is even greater courage to venture into positions or overcome situations that nobody like you, has gone to before or where many better qualified than you had gone and failed. In all cases, they all display courage in the face of obstacles and uncertainties. The success is more about courage than the experience. Can such courage be learned or inspired? How do leaders or successful people in their callings get to their heights of achievements? How can courage be an inner strength within or beyond leadership? How does courage attribute triumph over paralyzing fear? This course explores answers to these questions and more by searching for the distinguishing characteristics of courage. Numerous techniques, personal examples, empirical case studies, including practice questions at the end of each chapter are used to guide your development and to frame meanings out of the content to improve your acts of courage leadership process.

ALS II Course 3: Empathy Leadership Attribute—*A measure of a leader's compassion is the empathic engagement in a follower's experience and state of well-being beyond just expressions of feelings and concerns.*

Empathy attribute is the ability to project one's personality and experiences into another person's thoughts, emotions, direct experience, position, and act toward the wellness of that person. How can a leader walk along with someone in that individual's "wilderness" state of suffering or danger? What motivates a leader to *empathize* with a follower? How is empathy an inner strength leadership attribute? Whether it's in your church, your business, your institution, or in your community, this course provides a comprehensive biblical-based discussion on the role of a leader as a servant in empathizing with those he leads. The aim is to inspire the reader spiritually, mentally, and professionally with this far-reaching exposition on empathy in servant leadership. How can a leader make a lasting positive impact in the lives of those he or she leads? Answers to these and other personal reflective questions are explored in this course on Leadership Empathy Attributes. Numerous techniques, personal examples, empirical case studies, including practice questions at the end of each chapter are used to guide your development and to frame meanings out of the content to improve your acts of empathy leadership process.

ALS II Course 4: Encouragement Leadership Attribute—*The direct measures of encouragement are the inspired strength and quality of uplifted spirit to persevere toward a desired outcome.*

There are times when people want to grow in their potential, want to change their present situation, feel emotionally low in lived experiences, or feel as if they should be appreciated for a job well done. In any of these cases, some encouragement goes a long way to lift up the spirit of someone low. A case study is of the leadership qualities of Barnabas, named the "Son of Encouragement" by the disciples (Acts 4:36), because they saw him as an *encourager*. You can only be an encourager from the strength of your inner personality. The act of encouragement is mostly expressed or *given* to inspire growth or apply a spiritual gift to serve others. What did the disciples see in Barnabas? Obviously, he must have affected them with his acts of encouragement. They saw him as an encourager by his *courage* to *inspire* them at a time they desperately needed to move the ministry forward. This course explores the distinguishing characteristics of encouragement attributes in servant leadership. Each characteristic of encouragement attribute will be discussed in detail with emphasis on strategies of how they can be further developed or practiced by a leader-servant in a leadership process. Practice questions at the end of each chapter are used to guide your development and to frame meanings out of the content to improve your acts of encouragement leadership process.

ALS II Course 5: Initiation Leadership Attribute—*Initiation creates the catalyst for a vision, and the vision when acted upon, produces a desired change.*

The initiation of a process for a desired change is the core of the inner strength of a decisive leader in any leadership process. Initiation leadership is the act of taking step to originate or get something started. In general, initiative is an "individual's action that begins a process, often done without direct managerial influence." The primary outcome of the initiation attribute is that it leads to desired change; something new in the lives of the followers or organization, such as a new growth in followers, a new product or policy in an organization, or a new mission or mission agenda. How do leaders take action to begin a process of change? What are the distinguishing initiation characteristics of leaders such as Moses and Nehemiah in working according to God's agenda? How does a leader conceive a strategic vision for initiation action?. or negotiate his way to influence possible actions toward that vision. This course explores answers to these, and other questions based on examples from Nehemiah (Nehemiah 1:4 through 2:6-8) and Moses and God (Exodus 3 and 4:1-14).

ALS II Course 6: Listening Communication Leadership Attribute —*Effective communication occurs at the convergence of listening attention, hearing, and understanding of the information transmitted.*

A leader-servant face three important types of communication at one point or the other. At the core is listening ability as the inner strength and ability to receive and understand the meanings of words and messages internally and accurately in a two-way communication process. How does a leader-servant communication with God, the Holy Spirit, and followers (individually or collectively) to be most effective. The course explores how the three elements—words spoken, unspoken, and in the spirit—offer unique reflections of the communication process and what they share in common. How does listening serve as a critical element of effective communication between people forms the bridge by which a leader can be effective?. A leader's capacity to listen to communicate effectively depends on the leader's inner strength to perceive, hear, and understand the information from written, verbal, and non-verbal exchanges. Each characteristic of listening communications attribute will be discussed in detail with emphasis on strategies of how they can be further developed or practiced by a leader-servant. Practice questions at the end of each chapter are used to guide your development and to frame meanings out of the content to improve your acts of listening leadership process.

ALS II Course 7: Navigation Leadership Attribute—*Leaders who prepare for and chart through a purposeful course of action arrive with their followers at the desired destination.*

The navigation attribute is having a *vision* for the intended destination plus the direction to get there. Having a vision is a quality of the inner strength of a leader and the path that the leader follows in the life journey is often influenced by internal and external factors. The organizational culture and climate collectively combine to make an organization unique through the diversity of employees' characteristics, values, needs, attitudes, and expectations. How does a leader-servant *navigate* and *negotiate* his actions through the organization and people he serves, individually or collectively, to *finish* or *arrive* at his purpose? How do you prepare your followers to *finish* strong or *arrive* at their destinations? This course explores answers to these and other questions and how a leader's inner strength capacity can empower him to navigate the cultural bridges to influence the desired change in others in their personal and professional needs and attitudes.

ALS II Course 8: Responsibility Leadership Attribute—*Leadership responsibility is the measure of the quality of a Leader's accountability for the growth of followers and the organization*

Responsibility leadership refers to possessing the capability and accountability needed in the act of being responsible (trustworthy, dependable, honest, etc.) in a leadership process. At a personal level, it defines the level of your position (pastor, deacon, department head, janitor, etc.) in your church, family, or employment. Responsible leaders in their positions *choose* to emphasize the positive, uplifting, and flourishing side of organizational life. Are there qualities in your position that need to be trained or developed to influence positive outcomes in people and organizations? Organizationally, what are the attributes of the leadership structure, process, and culture that are most conducive for maximizing the growth of followers and organizations in service toward others? How can responsibility qualities be developed to enhance high-quality relationships, emotional competencies, positive communication, beneficial energy development, and positive climates for the effective leader as a servant leadership process? The course explores answers to these and other questions. Distinguishing leadership characteristics of responsibility attributes are identified and discussed in detail. Practice questions at the end of each chapter are used to guide your development and to frame meanings out of the content to improve your acts of responsibility leadership process.

ALS II Course 9: Stewardship Leadership Attribute—*A measure of good stewardship is the entrustments' better and richer growth change at the end than at the beginning*

***Stewardship leadership is the process of u**tilizing* and managing the resources entrusted to you by someone. We recognize that God has ownership of everything above, and below the earth. In that context, we are all stewards of what God owns, including our lives but entrusted to us to be managed and maintained in a purposeful manner that will honor God. What are the distinctive servant leadership characteristics of stewardship and how can they be developed? This course explores answers to these questions with reference to servant leadership. Practice questions at the end of each chapter are used to guide your development and to frame meanings out of the content to improve your acts of steward leadership process

ALS II Course 10: Vision Leadership Attribute—*You have a vision when you understand how you get to your mission-purpose and what the future outcome will be relative to your present.*

The vision leadership attribute gives the leader the ability to specify in the present *what* each follower's or group's growth should be in the future, *where* to focus these efforts to meet that growth; *how* he will accomplish all aspects of his mission, *which* future (destination) he aspires to lead the people, and *when* the purpose will be achieved. Leadership without direction leads followers to nowhere. Vision is the most common descriptor of effective leadership and must be clear and inspirational in order to achieve desired purpose. What are the qualities a visionary leader? When was the last time you added brand new challenges to your normal routine to achieve a new you? Answers to these and other questions are explored in this course. The primary characteristics of visionary leadership will be identified and used to frame a principle of leadership vision attribute. Practice questions at the end of each chapter are used to guide your development and to frame meanings out of the content to improve your acts of encouragement leadership process.

Referenced Scriptures

A variety of Bible translations from over 11,200 original Hebrew, Aramaic, and Greek words to about 6,000 English words do exist with variations in meanings and emphases. I am not a biblical scholar and do not pretend to be one; Hence, I have avoided researching the roots of these words and personally prefer New King James Version (NKJV). I have intentionally used other translations for three main reasons; first, to allow for increased impact and alignment of words to the most desired meaning and emphasis in the concepts being addressed. Second, I wanted new and personal discovery of meanings from translations with which I have not been familiar. And third, I wanted to allow readers who may desire translations other than the NKJV the benefit of their preferred translations. Hence, in addition to the NKJV, other translations used in the book include New International Version (NIV), New Living Translation (NLT), King James Version (KJV), English Standard Version (ESV), and Good News Translation (GNT). Unless otherwise specified, NKJV should be assumed.

Sylvanus Nwakanma Wosu

CHAPTER 1
UNDERSTANDING LEADERSHIP ATTRIBUTES

Leadership attribute is the combined acts of two or more distinctive functional leadership characteristics exhibited in service and relationship toward others.

The starting point of our discussion is the understanding of the key functional definitions and concepts that describe the theme of this book. In general, 1 will define leadership as an integrative process in which a person applies appropriate attributes to guide and influence the sought-after attitudinal changes in others toward accomplishing a particular goal. Specifically, the Leader as Servant Leadership is a process in which a leader intentionally chooses to put the follower's rights and needs above his positional rights and personal needs, and serves, enables, and empowers them for desired spiritual and professional growth that builds thriving communities.

FUNCTIONAL DEFINITIONS

In the context of these definitions, I will begin the descriptions of the leadership attributes of an authentic leader-servant by offering a functional definition of Leadership Attributes, and showing how that definition differs from those of Leadership Character, Characteristics, and Traits.

Leadership Character is the sum total of personal qualities in leadership, such as honesty, values, vision, trust, and so on that make up the moral capital of the leader; Leadership character should describe who the leader is inside or the leader's basic personality traits.

The Leadership Characteristics describe the distinctive characteristics or features of a leader, such as attitudes, competencies, skills, and specific experiences that go beyond his character (personality). Leadership characteristics determine how (through skills and competencies) the leader leads or take actions in the process of leadership in any particular situation;

The Leadership traits are the distinguishing leadership characteristics of a leader (these are things that define his leadership characteristics), which differentiate from personality traits... Leadership traits are the set of characteristics that define a particular leader's leadership. This means that a leadership characteristic is a trait when it is a unique characteristic of the leader.

Leadership Attributes, unlike leadership character, characteristics, and traits, is *a leadership attribute and the combined act of two or more distinctive functional leadership characteristics exhibited in service and relationship toward others* or traits externally displayed in action toward others. All leadership attributes grow out of the leadership inner value system but can be externally displayed predominantly as an outbound or outward attribute or both:

1. **Outbound Attributes:** These are distinctive outward-bound attributes emanating from the inner strength of the leader to support external conduct in service and relationships toward others. They form the internal core functional qualities that motivate or enhance the outward manifestation of the inside character toward others. The outbound attribute such as listening and vision, for example, are the direct results of the inner values of the leader such as patience, hearing, love, humility, or all the fruits of the spirit.

2. **Outward Attributes:** These are distinctive functional outward outer visible attributes emanating from the richness of the outbound and inner values of the leader. For example, external attributes such as Servanthood, emulation/modeling, empathy, etc. are outflows from the leader who will directly impact the follower. Outward attributes can be enriched by the outbound (inner) attributes. As shown in Figure 1, the outward attributes in general form the outer core of

CHAPTER 1
UNDERSTANDING LEADERSHIP ATTRIBUTES

functional attributes in the leader as servant leadership, but they can share some overlapping functions with the outbound attributes.

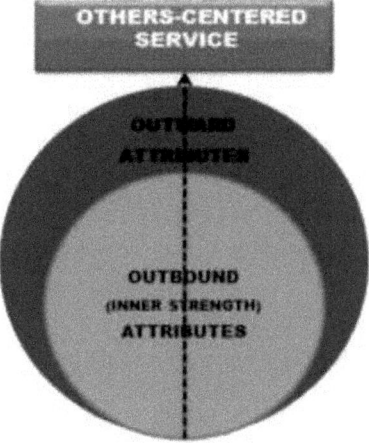

Figure 1.1. Servant leadership functional attributes

In summary, a leadership attribute is more than an ability or a characteristic; it is making those characteristics or abilities functional as part of how the leader acts (his habits) in service to others and applying those characteristics (beyond just having them) in personal and service relations to others. The character or known characteristic defines some aspects of your abilities or who you are inside— e.g. honest, humble, brave, etc. Your attribute, on the other hand, defines your habits; a display of how you use your characteristics, or the actions you exhibit toward others because of who you are inside. For example, empathy as a leadership characteristic becomes a leadership attribute if the followers can distinguish the leader's acts or habits of empathy, such as walking through with his followers in their state of suffering to bring wholeness; otherwise, it is just a characteristic or ability. Leadership attributes toward others are what impact the followers' and the organizational growth more than ability and competence.

In addressing one of the self-righteous hypocritical attributes of servitude leadership, Jesus called leader-servants to be "inside-out" leaders that reflect credibility; indeed, leaders should not appear outwardly righteous when they are full of hypocrisy and lawlessness in their hearts. He was describing "inside–out" as an authentic leadership attribute measured by the display of credibility a leadership attribute!

The measuring stick of a leader-servant is Jesus Christ. We measure ourselves unto the measure of the status of the fullness of Christ (Ephesians 4:13).

The leadership attributes of an authentic leader as a servant are encapsulated in **SERVANT/SERVING LEADERSHIP** are listed in Table 1.1, and defined in Table 1.2: *Servanthood, Emulation, Responsibility, Vision, Navigation, Adaptability, Trust, Listening, Empathy, Affection, Discipleship, Encouragement, Reproduction, Stewardship, Healing-Care, Initiation, Integrity,* and *Persuasion*. Other support attributes include *Influence, Courage, and Generosity*.

The attributes have been separated into Outward and Outbound (Inner Strength) leadership Attributes. As shown in Table 1.1, each of these attributes has three or more leadership characteristics. As such, more than 65 leadership characteristics are covered in these 20 attributes. For example, a leader's Servanthood leadership attribute is characterized by his willing servant's heart of selfless role humility, sacrifice, and submissiveness. The more these are present in a leader, the more effective the servant leadership.

Table 1.1: The functional leader-servant leadership Outbound (Inner Strength) and Outward attributes

	LEADER-SERVANT LEADERSHIP ATTRIBUTES			INNER STRENGTH ATTRIBUTES	OUTWARD ATTRIBUTES
S	Servanthood	L	Listening	Adaptability	Affection
E	Emulation	E	Empathy	Courage	Discipleship
R	Responsibility	A	Affection	Empathy	Emulation
V	Vision	D	Discipleship	Encouragement	Generosity
A	Adaptability	E	Encouragement	Initiation	Healing-Care
N	Navigation	R	Reproduction	Listening	Influence
T	Trust	S	Stewardship	Navigation	Persuasion
I	Influence	H	Healing-Care	Responsibility	Reproduction
G	Generosity	I	Initiation	Stewardship	Servanthood
C	Courage	P	Persuasion	Vision	Trust/Integrity

The list does not assume that a leader has to be excellent in all attributes or even have all of them to be an effective Leader–Servant. However, the more of these attributes the leader displays in his acts of service toward others, the more productive he or she will be, and the further his impact on the followers and organization. The table also shows that two or more attributes can share common characteristics, which can be applied or observed in different contexts. For example, a leader's ability to inspire followers can be seen in his acts of discipleship, empowerment, an.d encouragement attributes in the context in which these attributes apply. Each attribute is exhibited either as a part of the outbound inner strength attribute of a leader or a part of the outward attribute. Table 1.1 is not an exhaustive list of attributes; in fact, there are hundreds of such attributes. This is just the starting point.

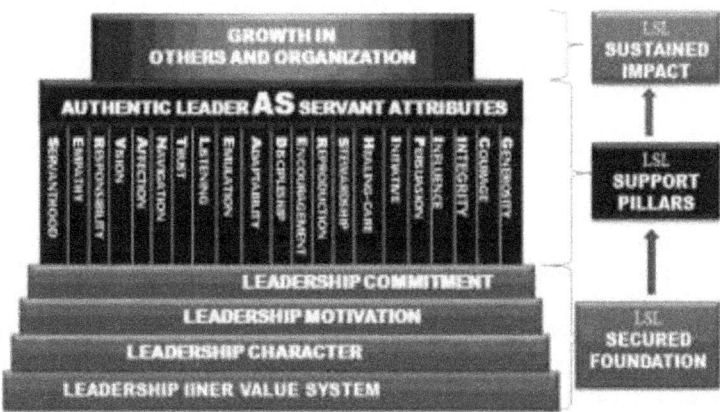

Figure 1.2: Servant leadership outward attributes (dark blue) and relationship to four foundational layers of the LSL Model

Figure 1.2 shows that the leader's attributes are shaped and secured by his four foundational layers (leadership inner value system, leadership character, motivation, and commitment). The attributes of the leader–servants are also conceptualized as the support pillars that will establish and support the personal authenticity of the leader, what the leader, does and the effectiveness of the leadership process. Thus, the attributes represent functional pillars of authentic leadership that can be learned or enriched as described in detail in the subsequent chapters. The combined effect of a secured foundation and stable support pillars will make a sustained impact on the growth of followers and the organization.

COMPARISONS WITH OTHER WORKS

The original works by Greenleaf (1970) in servant leadership [1] have been reviewed by Larry Spears (1996), who identified listening, empathy, healing, awareness, persuasion, conceptualization, foresight, stewardship, commitment to the growth of others, and building community as the ten distinguishing characteristics of servant leadership. [2] Russell (2001) has studied these attributes and have shown them to be essential in servant leadership and concluded that these qualities generally "grow out of the inner values and beliefs of individual leaders." [3] Russell and Stone (2002) extended the Greenleaf 10 attributes to 20 attributes observed in servant-leaders. These 20 attributes were categorized by these authors as either functional attributes (intrinsic characteristics of servant-leaders) or accompanying attributes (complement attributes that enhance the functional attributes).[4] The operational attributes were identified as vision, honesty, integrity, trust, modeling, service, pioneering, appreciation, and empowerment with the accompanying attributes of communication, credibility, competence, stewardship, visibility, influence, persuasion, listening, encouragement, teaching, and delegation. Only three of the attributes identified by Greenleaf were identified, and all three were accompanying attributes rather than functional. Responsibility, adaptability, affection, discipleship, navigation, and reproduction attributes which are considered critical in biblical-based servant leadership in my LSL model are not covered by Russell and Greenleaf. As shown in the description of the attributes in Table 1.2, most of the attributes reported by Russell and Stone (2002)[5] or Greenleaf [1] can be seen either in the twenty attributes or their associated characteristics. Integrity and honesty for example are leadership characteristics of trust and other attributes rather than an independent attributes. I take the position that servant leadership attributes are functional attributes in acts of duty to others and emanate from the inner value system of the leader.

CHAPTER 1
UNDERSTANDING LEADERSHIP ATTRIBUTES

Table 1.2: Description of the functional leader-servant outward leadership attributes and associated principles and characteristics

Leader–Servant Leadership Attributes	Principles of Leadership Attributes	Leadership Characteristics
Affection: *This is the combined love-based works toward providing the essential help or services for the spiritual growth or survival of another person. .* (Chapter 2)	*Affection flows from a person to produce positive emotions for the well-being of another person*	Kindness Compassion Practical Love Affective signs Appreciation
Discipleship: *This is the combined acts of personally developing, intentionally equipping, and attentively empowering growth in others to reproduce a heart of service.* (Chapter 3)	*Discipleship transforms and empowers followers for service leadership that grows communities.*	Inspiring Shepherding Equipping Developing Empowering
Emulation: *This is the combined acts of initiating an authentic servant attitude as a model of service worthy of following* (Chapter 4)	*A great leader-servant outwardly and positively inspires a pattern of good works for others to follow.*	Inspiration Motivation Initiation Model Following
Generosity: *This is the combined acts of freely sharing with and giving to others as an act of kindness, without expectation of reward or return to him.* (Chapter 5)	*Generosity is an outward measure of the level of sacrifice, what is shared, or the impact a giving makes, not just the size of the giving.*	Sharing Giving Kindness Affection Love
Healing-Care: *This is the combined acts of providing comfort and empathy to make others whole emotionally and spiritually along with tending to the follower's physical and mental well-being.* (Chapter 6)	*Comforting others in any trouble with the comfort with which we are comforted by God, brings healing - wholeness.*	Self-Healing Empathy Reconciliation Comfort Relational
Influence: *This is the combined acts of positively affecting desired change in conduct,*	*The true measure of leadership success in affecting*	Model Positive attitude Authority

performance, and relational connections toward others-centered course of action or service. (Chapter 7)	desired change in conduct, performance, and relational connections in others is influence	Connection Wisdom Intelligence,
Persuasion: *This is the combined acts of communicating perspective to connect, challenge, and convince with a compelling purpose to convert others to a new position.* (Chapter 8)	*The means of transforming others to a new perspective is through empathetic persuasion*	Connecting Challenging Communicating Convincing Converting Encouraging
Reproduction: *This is the combined acts of developing your leadership qualities in others and releasing them as successors to continue a greater mission.* (Chapter 9)	*Great leaders produce successors for legacy and greater courses as an expected product of an effective leadership reproduction.*	Selecting Mentoring Equipping Empowering Releasing
Servanthood: *This is the combined acts of humility, willingness, and intentionality in service to others through selfless sacrifice and submission as a servant.* (Chapter 10)	*A leader-servant is most qualified to lead when most ready to serve as a servant for the growth of others. The role of a leader is to serve as a servant*	Servant's heart Humility Sacrifice Service Willingness Submissiveness
Trust: *This is the combined acts of positive display of character, competence, credibility, and shared relational connections that produce assured trust-confidence of the trustee in the trusted.* (Chapter 11)	*True leadership trust produces assured trustee's confidence and readiness to follow based on the credibility, competence, and shared relational connections of the trusted.*	Character Competence Integrity Credibility Confidence

PRINCIPLE OF LEADERSHIP ATTRIBUTE

In the context of servant leadership, a leadership attribute is a level above the leadership characteristic or trait of a leader. The principle of leadership attribute states that every leadership attribute has a set of distinguishing characteristics that make up the inward or outward display of the attribute. The principle reflects the essential designed purpose or outcome of the attribute or the inevitable consequence of the effective practice of the attribute. Thus, the principle of leadership attribute is a concise statement about the fundamental truth, value, or belief about the attribute in a leadership situation; it is a statement that establishes an idea about the outcome of the attribute for guiding the practical application of the attribute and its characteristics. I will postulate and frame each principle as an additive function of the characteristics of the attribute. A statement of each principle is quoted at the beginning or below the title of each chapter. It is yet to be experimentally proven if the attribute is a linear or some other non-linear function of these characteristics as variables. It is expected, however, that each character will contribute to the effectiveness of the attribute in varying degrees.

AUTHENTIC LEADERSHIP ATTRIBUTES

At a personal level, attributes are the value-based inside-out moral leadership assets that can be related to the authenticity of a leader-servant. The complexity of defining authenticity has been noted in the literature. The subject of authentic leadership is well covered in the works of Terry (1993),[5] George (2003),[6] and Shair and Eilam (2005).[7] All appear to agree that authenticity requires self-awareness and objective self-identity in personal and social interactions with others. In his book, *Advocacy Leadership*, Professor Gary L. Anderson offers individual, organizational, and societal perspectives on authenticity: "Authenticity, at a peculiar level, is living a life, whether in the private or professional term. This is congruent with one's espoused values; at the structural level, authenticity has to do with viewing human beings as ends in themselves, rather than means to other ends; at the public level, it is a state of affairs that is congruous with the shared political and cultural values of society." [8]

The basic tenets of these perspectives are very fitting to authenticity as a qualifying element of leader-servant leadership attributes. The attribute reflects how the followers see the leader based on the leader's distinctive features displayed through his or her actions personally, organizationally, and societally. The leader is seen as a leader-servant or serving leader because the followers see him lead as a servant from an inside-out value of others. This is what makes the leader authentic.

Authenticity means that what a leader displays outside, in personal or leadership life of service to others, and society is based on the values the leader espouses inside.

Authenticity in servant leadership can be one or two types or both: *Outbound Authenticity and Outward Authenticity*: The Outbound (outward-bound) Authenticity is the genuineness of personal honesty from your inner strength and abilities; what you say and how you act emanate from who you are or how you feel inside. It reflects the essential truth and honesty about your outward-bound inner strength.

Outward authenticity, on the other hand, describes the truthfulness of your credibility and honesty displayed outward in relation to others; your *outer* visible behavior or how you act outwardly towards others reflects exactly your true intentions.

While *outward* authenticity is the visible *outer* indicator of the truth of who you are inside, *outbound* authenticity is outward-bound attribute from the inside of who you are. Credibility in this context is the influence a leader has to attract believability, trustworthiness, and authenticity; it is the believability, trustworthiness, and authenticity of who you are inside and outside.

A key element of personal authenticity is that it is seen or measured in the context of societal, cultural, and organizational interactions. In that context, achieving individual authenticity becomes a challenge since it is influenced by social factors and dispositions of individuals who usually depend on liberal and organizational realities. However, for leader-servant leadership, the leader can face those changing times by remaining focused on his key Biblical-based principles or *Leadership Inner Value System*. Thus, I am interested in authenticity as an essential element of effective Leader-servant leadership attributes or Leader-servant leadership attributes as drivers of leadership authenticity. With that in mind, the first critical element of authenticity in practicing or developing efficient leader-servant leadership attributes is inside-out self-examination relative to the people served rather than the organization. You may ask yourself: What will be my response when the people I lead act or react in a certain way, will it be negative or positive? What are my strengths and vulnerabilities at those times?

Professor Yacobi in his post, "Elements of Human Authenticity," noted that since "the self -arise attribute emerges from interactions between self, others, and the environment in a complex society and world, there may co-exist multiple complicated identities depending on place and context." [9] He went on to identify the following <u>essential elements of personal authenticity</u>: self-awareness, unbiased self-examination, accurate self-knowledge, reflective judgment, personal responsibility, and integrity, genuineness, and humility, empathy for others, understanding of others, optimal utilization of feedback from others. All of these are covered under the leadership attributes or characteristics shown in Table 1.2.

Bill George, in his book, *Authentic Leadership*, takes the position that to be an authentic leader; a person must have the following essential characteristics: [10]

- Behavior based on value: He must understand his own values and exhibit behavior to others based on those values;
- He must not compromise his values in difficult situations but could use the situation to strengthen personal values in those situations.
- Passion from a clear purpose: Be self-aware of who he is, where he is going, and the right thing to do.
- Compassion from the heart: He must lead from a compassionate heart that allows them to be sensitive to the plight and needs of others,
- Connectedness from a relationship; he must be relationally connected with people he leads,
- Consistency from the self-disciple: He must demonstrate self-discipline to remain calm, collected, and consistent in a stressful situation.

Modeled after the elements above, Table 1.3 lists six essential characteristics of authenticity for servant leadership. These fundamental characteristics cover the five identified above and can also be aligned with the leadership characteristics in Table 1.2. Each attribute in Table 1.2 is expected to pass the personal authenticity test in Tables 1.3, 1.4. In a survey of 132 Christian leaders, seventy-four percent (74%) of them agreed that they always or frequently exhibit servant leadership attributes. [11] Thus, a pass of the outward authenticity test means that a pure leader must demonstrate 70% or more of these essential elements of this legitimacy. (That is, 70% YES in the assessment questions in Tables 1.3, 1.4).

It needs to be noted, however, that a secular leader could be authentic and still lack some of the essential servant leadership attributes or characteristics such as selflessness, servanthood, and love-motivated servant attitudes of a leader-servant. Effective leader-servants are authentic leaders and personal authenticity is an essential element of leader-servant leadership. The key test for leader-servant authenticity is the quality of his inside-out value and personal character. What is most important is a change from the inside-out.

Table 1.3: The test of essential elements of personal inner strength authenticity in servant leadership

	Elements of Inner Strength Authenticity	Inner Strength (Outbound) Authenticity Assessment Questions	YES / NO
1	Personal inside-out value-based behavior	Are your personal inside-out values aligned with acts of service and behavior outside?	1
		Are you honest to yourself in relation to your inner strengths and abilities?	2
2	Inside-out Self-Awareness	Do you have unbiased self-examination, and accurate self-knowledge of who you are inside-out?	3
		Do you know your inner strength and weaknesses in relation to the good you want to show as an outward attribute?	4
3	Inside-out Empathy-Compassion	Do you know and feel from your inside what you want for your followers?	5
		Are you motivated to empathize, based on your inside feelings?	6
4	Inside-out Connection with followers	Do you feel deep, personal, and spiritual connection with your followers?	7
		Does what you say and how you act reflect how you feel when you relate to others?	8
5	Inside-out Emotional Self-regulation	Do you have difficulty controlling your emotion in order to remain calm in a stressful situation?	9
		Are you always able to comfort yourself?	10
6	Inside-out Authenticity Feedback	Do your followers see your inside-out value from your outside behavior?	11
		Will your followers feel that what you say you are is congruent with how you act?	12
#YESs_____ ; # NOs_____ : Outbound Authenticity: YES/ 12-----%			

Table 1.4: The test of essential elements of personal outward authenticity in servant leadership

	Elements of Personal Outward Authenticity	Personal Outward Authenticity Assessment Questions	YES or NO
1	Personal value-based outward behavior	Are your personal values and beliefs aligned with your acts of service and behavior toward others?	1
		Do you live out your life according to your beliefs?	2
2	Personal Self-Awareness	Do you have clarity of your personal vision and purpose?	3
		Does what you know about yourself accurately describe what others say?	4
3	Personal Outward Empathy-Compassion	Do you apply how you feel to what your followers need?	5
		Do you lead from a compassionate heart and are you sensitive to the plight and needs of others?	6
4	Personal Connection with followers	Do you feel deep, personal connection with your followers?	7
		Does your outward action toward others reflect exactly your true intentions?	8
5	Outward Emotional Self-regulation	Do you have difficulty controlling your emotions to remain calm in a stressful situation?	9
		Does your evaluation of your value of others agree with how valued they feel?	10
6	Personal Authenticity Feedback	Do your followers see your outward acts as true and honest?	11
		Can your followers see other-centeredness in 70% or more of your attributes?	12
#YESs____; # NOs____: Outbound Authenticity: YES/ 12-----%			

SUMMARY 1
UNDERSTANDING LEADERSHIP PROCESS

Before starting this exercise, please read and follow the instruction in the preface of this workbook. Answers to these questions are contained in this chapter. Completion of these exercises after reading the chapter should take 60-90 minutes.

Discovering the Leadership Attributes

1. What is your alternative definition of leadership? In learning to lead, how would you differentiate the following elements:
    a. Leadership.
    b. Leader as servant leadership.
    c. Leadership characteristics.
    d. Leadership attributes.
2. What are the key differences between the Leader as Servant and the Servant as Leader Leadership philosophies?
3. What was the original source of the Servant as Leader (SL)? What was the original source of Leader as Servant (LS)?
4. What is the key framework of a Leader as a Servant Leadership?
5. Authenticity in servant leadership can be one or two types or both *Outbound Authenticity and Outward Authenticity*: Describe a time when you displayed:
    a. The Outbound (outward-bound)—*outbound* authenticity is outward-bound attribute from the inside of who you are.
    b. *The Outward Authenticity*—*outward* authenticity is the visible *outer* indicator of the truth of who you are inside,
6. Describe the key elements of personal authenticity seen or measured in the context of societal, cultural, and organizational interactions.
7. How are the essential characteristics of authentic leader in leadership process in challenging times?
8. How much of a leader-servant are you? Take the personal leader-servant audit in Table 1.5 to self-assess your effectiveness.
9. Based on the questions in Table 1.5, can you identify each of the twenty attributes? What ones did you score 3 ("sometimes") or less than 3? Review and learn and commit to work to improve.

CHAPTER 1
UNDERSTANDING LEADERSHIP ATTRIBUTES

Table 1.5. Leader As Servant-Leadership Audit

A servant-leader in his leadership position purposefully choses to serve and inspire acts of service in others by his example. Select and circle best answer to questions
1=Never: 2=Almost never; 3=Sometimes; 4=Frequently; 5 =Always

	Servant Leadership assessment questions	Circle no				
1	I am willing and other-centered, and readily chose to serve others as a servant for their personal growth	1	2	3	4	5
2	I model others-centered attitude in my service and relationships and inspire same for others to follow	1	2	3	4	5
3	I have a sense of obligation, willingness, and accountability for the service towards others	1	2	3	4	5
4	I have the foresightedness to specify in the present view what others' growth should be in a given future	1	2	3	4	5
5	I work toward providing the essential help or services for the spiritual growth or survival of the others;	1	2	3	4	5
6	I provide the needed purposeful course of action for how to chart the course to for my followers.	1	2	3	4	5
7	I display external credibility and a strong sense of character based on values, beliefs, and competence;	1	2	3	4	5
8	In communication, I attentively perceive and hear what is communicated, reflectively listen to understand and to be understood	1	2	3	4	5
9	I walk through with others in their state (suffering, emotions, etc.) in a way that provides the needed care and well-being	1	2	3	4	5
10	I have a measure of self-secured flexibility to adapt appropriate attitude to serve all people in different situations	1	2	3	4	5
11	I personally develop, intentionally equip, and attentively nurture spiritually growth in others	1	2	3	4	5
12	My act of bravery instills in others the courage and confidence to follow or persevere in a course of action	1	2	3	4	5
13	I develop my leadership qualities in others as successors to continue in a purposeful mission	1	2	3	4	5
14	I manage, maintain,, and account for all resources entrusted to me and being responsible for the difference my acts make	1	2	3	4	5
15	As a care-giver, I act to comfort and make others whole emotionally	1	2	3	4	5
16	When I see a need, I originate a vision and action, and stay committed to meet that need and desired change	1	2	3	4	5

ALS EMPATHY LEADERSHIP
ATTRIBUTES, PRINCIPLES, & PRACTICES

17	I display a holistic view of an issue to inform, transform or convert others to my view through empathetic persuasion	1	2	3	4	5
18	I freely share what I have sacrificially as an act of kindness to others, without expectation of reward in return	1	2	3	4	5
19	My act of influence is to affect the actions, behavior, opinions, etc., of others based on trust, credibility and relationship	1	2	3	4	5
20	In the face challenges and danger, I act with bravery to overcome fear and take a stand with strength and conviction	1	2	3	4	5
Score Range	Add up the numbers in each column (Total Score____ Check and Understand the key areas to work on					
81-100	Strong Leader-Servant; keep it up, go and train others.					
66-80	Above average Leader-Servant; work 25% of key areas					
50-65	Average but developing; need to work on 50% of key areas					
34-49	Below average leader; work on 75% of key areas					
<34	Not a Leader-Servant; need training in all areas					

CHAPTER 2
EMPATHY LEADERSHIP ATTRIBUTE

A measure of a leader's compassion is the empathic engagement in a follower's experience and state of well-being beyond just expressions of feelings and concerns

How can a leader walk along with someone in that individual's "wilderness" state of suffering or danger? What motivates a leader to *empathize* with a follower? How is empathy an inner strength leadership attribute? Whether it's in your church, your business, your institution, or in your community, this chapter provides a comprehensive biblical-based discussion on the role of a leader as a servant in empathizing with those he leads. The aim is to inspire the reader spiritually, mentally, and professionally with this far-reaching exposition on empathy in servant leadership. How can a leader make a lasting positive impact in the lives of those he or she leads? Daniel Goleman, a leading American psychologist, lists empathy as one of the five elements of emotional intelligence (defined as "the ability to understand and manage both your own emotions, and those of the people around you") [12] Goleman shows that people with a high degree of emotional intelligence usually know what they're feeling, what the feelings mean, and how their emotions can affect other people. [12] Other elements of emotional intelligence include self-awareness, self-regulation, motivation, and social skills. How are these characteristics related to servant leadership? Answers to these and other personal reflective questions are explored in this chapter on Leadership Empathy Attributes. Functional definitions of leadership empathy attributes and principles will be provided based on the identified characteristics. Readers will benefit from numerous techniques, personal examples, empirical case studies, and applications of the concepts.

SERVANT LEADERSHIP EMPATHY ATTRIBUTE

Empathy is an innate personal caring act in which a person gives undivided attention to someone else's experience in a way that makes the other person feel that they both share and understand the essential elements of an experience. You feel empathy when you've "been there." Here, I refer to this type of empathy as personal empathy. Personal empathy is an inner strength quality of a leader-servant that gives him or her, the required sympathy, compassion, and responsiveness to care for a follower in a way that builds that person up in that experience. One can only project a personality known, has, and can control. Hence, I will take *self-awareness* as an element of empathy.

Personal empathy involves a deeper level of *emotional* experience. The functional element is the ability to feel emotional or be self-aware of what the other person is going through because you have had the same or a similar experience or can somehow relate to that experience. An experience of an event in the context of empathy is not a function of just being in or seeing that event. It occurs when one can make valid sense out of the experience by projecting oneself into the experience or sharing in a similar experience.

Empathy sympathy is the kind of sympathy that leads to empathy. It is the beginning of concern and the feeling level of empathy. Sympathy is feeling concerned and caring that the needs of others are met. Empathy and sympathy have similar uses but are very different in meaning and application. One's level of sympathy depends on the varying state of needs, pain, vulnerability, and danger the sympathetic object feels. While sympathy involves expressing feelings and concerns for the well-being of another person without sharing any specific emotional state, empathy involves self-awareness, understanding, and sharing a specific emotional state with another person. [13] The emphasis in sympathy is *awareness* or understanding of another person's situation that deserves attention because of an element of pain, suffering, or loss that the person is experiencing.

Compassion is another characteristic of empathy; it is the perceptive engagement or responsive stage of empathy. Empathy-compassion is the action level of empathy and it manifests when one shows feelings and concerns (sympathy); shares deep emotional experiences with a care-receiver (empathy), and takes further action (compassion) to meet the need or ease the person's suffering. Compassion as an empathetic dimension of a leader-servant involves putting oneself in the other person's shoes and taking action to help ease their pain, not just feeling or showing concern. Researchers on human emotions generally agree that compassion is a feeling in response to another person's state of suffering that motivates action to relieve that suffering.

God is our ultimate empathizer because he knows us more than we know ourselves. David said, "For He knows our frame; He remembers that we are dust" (Psalm 103:14, NKJV) How comforting it is to know that God records all our tears as we struggle in our lives! "The LORD is close to the brokenhearted and saves those who are crushed in spirit" (Psalm 34:18, NIV). This is David's way of expressing God's total empathy toward His children. Paul also uses some comforting words of sympathy, "Praise be to the God and Father of our Lord Jesus Christ, the Father of compassion and the God of all comfort, who comforts us in all our troubles so that we can comfort those in any trouble with the comfort we ourselves receive from God." (2 Corinthians 1:3-4). The abundant comfort we receive from Lord emanates from our inside and enables us to comfort others (2 Corinthians 1:5). All three levels of emotions: sympathy, compassion, and empathy relate to feelings but at different levels.

A leader-servant must be able to demonstrate empathy. The Apostle Peter said, "Compassion for one another; love as brothers, be tenderhearted, be courteous. "(*1 Peter 3:8*, NKJV). The Apostle Paul recommended similar sentiments when he exhorted fellow Christians to "Rejoice with those who rejoice, and weep with those who weep" (Romans 12:15, NKJV). This means to project oneself into the experience of those who rejoice and weep, or feel others' feelings. From the above background, five integrated inner strength elements of empathy emerge:

1. **Emotional experience**: The presence of past situations in which one experiences with another person in an emotional state that expresses his or her needs or exhibits some suffering.
2. **Awareness**: Self-awareness and an understanding of one's personality (thoughts, feelings, reactions, concerns, and motives).
3. **Sympathy**: Perceiving and expressing feelings and concerns for someone's sadness, grief, worry, or hopelessness, often expressing and desiring to help heal the hurting person.
4. **Emotional control** (self-regulation): the ability to "stay in control" of your own emotions and feelings as you walk in another's experiences and associated emotions.
5. **Compassion**: Engaging and responding to the needs of another with a focus on easing the pain or suffering of that person.

PRINCIPLE OF LEADERSHIP EMPATHY ATTRIBUTE

The empathy attribute can be the ability to project one's personality and experiences into another person's thoughts, emotions, direct experience, and position. However, it is not only the ability but personally acting on or using that ability toward the wellness of another person. Empathy attribute is the sum of the actions you take to walk through that other person's experience in a particular position. In all cases, the end goal is the well-being of another person. Hence, I posit the following:

> *Servant leadership empathy attribute is the combined acts of projecting oneself and experiences into another person's thoughts, emotions, and experiences to give needed care for that person's state of well-being.*

Developing effective empathy attributes requires developing each of the levels of empathetic characteristics. It requires humility at its core as demonstrated by Jesus. All five elements of empathy work in stages and are driven purely by humility at different levels, to establish the groundwork for compassion. This is summarized as follows:

CHAPTER 2
EMPATHY LEADERSHIP ATTRIBUTE

Servant leadership empathy principle: A measure of a leader's compassion is the empathic engagement in a follower's experience and state of well-being beyond just expressions of feelings and concerns.

This principle and attribute are modeled in Figure 2.1 as a progression of intentional actions leading to total empathy and expressed as a function of the characteristics:

SELF-AWARENESS + SYMPATHY + EMOTION + COMPASSION = EMPATHY

The principle means that empathy results when a leader, as a caregiver, intentionally engages himself to walk alongside another person to extend care. Leadership Empathy Attribute is effective in building up or healing a follower; usually, the follower can sense the impact of the leader walking along in the experience. Thus, an important measure of effectiveness is whether the care receiver or follower senses that the caregiver is relating empathetically with him or her. It is not enough to say that you have related emphatically to a person unless that person senses a direct impact of your action.

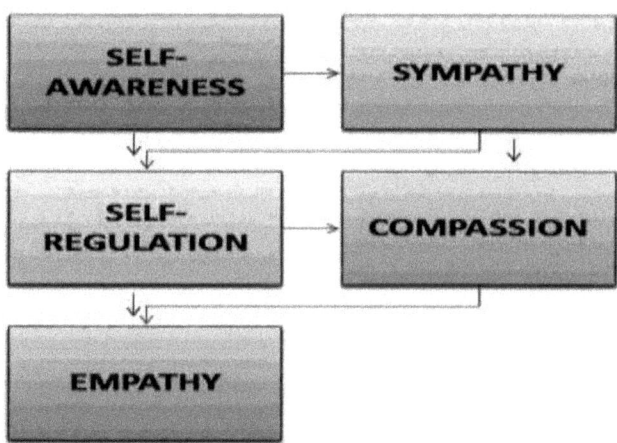

Figure 2.1: A four-stage Progression model of Servant leadership Empathy-attribute

Figure 3 shows it is possible to have cross-interaction among the levels. For example, one can move from self-awareness to emotional self-regulation without passing the sympathy level or from sympathy to compassion.

SUMMARY 2
EMPATHY LEADERSHIP ATTRIBUTE

Before starting this exercise, please read and follow the instruction in the preface of this workbook. Answers to these questions are contained in this chapter. Completion of these exercises after reading the chapter should take 60-90 minutes.

Discovering Empathy Leadership Attributes

1. Define empathy; what do you consider as the key elements of Empathy leadership?
2. How is empathy an inner strength leadership attribute? What is personal empathy and how would describe your personal empathy attributes?
3. Emotional intelligence is defined as "the ability to understand and manage both your own emotions, and those of the people around you") How is empathy an element of emotional intelligence?
4. What are other characteristics of empathy?
5. What does the Bible teach about empathy as shown by David in (Psalm 103:14, Psalm 34:18) or in Paul's letter (2 Corinthians 1:3-5; Romans 12:15) and Peter's teachings (*1 Peter 3:8*)?
6. What are the five integrated inner strength elements of empathy?

Understanding the Principle of Leadership Empathy Attribute

1. As a principle, empathy attribute is both the ability and personally acts or use of that ability toward the wellness of another person. What do you consider to be the end goal of empathy attribute?
2. Define Servant leadership empathy attribute
3. State Servant leadership empathy principle. What does this principle mean with rest to leadership?
4. State the additive law of empathy leadership attribute
Practicing Empathy Attribute

CHAPTER 2
EMPATHY LEADERSHIP ATTRIBUTE

Practicing Empathy Leadership -Attribute

1. What would you consider the key characteristics of the empathy leadership attribute?
2. How many acts of empathy as an attribute do you display?
3. Take the leadership empathy attribute audit in Table AII.3
4. Based on the questions in Table AII.3, can you identify each of the characteristics? What ones did you score 3 ("sometimes") or less than 3? Write a personal commitment how to improve in those areas.
5. Empathy occurs when a caregiver responds in practical terms (sacrifice, resources, and time) to meet the need of another person with a focus to ease the pain or suffering of that person.
    a) Explain how the five integrated elements of empathy lead to complete empathy toward a person.
    b) What are the three critical characteristics of empathy attribute?

Table AII.3. Leadership Empathy Attribute Audit

Servant leadership empathy attribute is the combined acts of projecting oneself and experiences into another person's thoughts, emotions, and experiences to give needed care for that person's state of well-being. Assess the quality of your acts of empathy attribute by inserting an X below the number that best describes your response to each statement.

Item	Acts of Empathy Attribute Check 1= Always; 2= Frequently; 3= Sometimes; 4: Almost Never; 5= Never	1	2	3	4	5
1	I act in practical ways to meet the need and ease the pain of others.					
2	I assess my actions, reactions, and general attitudes toward people					
3	I am able to catch myself in the moment prior to saying something destructive to others					
4	My act of compassion is given beyond just sympathy to bring wellness to a person.					
5	I am open to learn about myself by the way others perceive and respond to my acts					
6	My self-discipline during challenging times do yield dependence on God					
7	I usually walk along with someone in that person's state of wellbeing or suffering					
8	I act in ways that express my feelings and concern for others wellbeing					
9	I give proper undivided attention to the specific situation and need of others					
10	I act is ways to regulate and control my emotions to channel attention for the good of others					
	Add up your rating in each column					
Score Range	Guide and Explanation of Score: understand areas to develop	Total Score=				
10-17:	Great empathizer; keep it up					
18-25:	Above Average- empathizer; work on a few (25%) in some key					
26-33:	Average but developing empathy; work in 50% of key areas					
34-41:	Below average- empathizer; work on (75%) of the key areas					
42-50:	Not an empathizer ; work on all the key areas					

CHAPTER 3
DEVELOPING EMPATHY–
SELF AWARENESS ATTRIBUTE

Bruna Martinuzzi, the President of Clarion Enterprises Ltd., noted in her book, *The Leader as a Mensch: Become the Kind of Person Others Want to Follow*, that "Some people who are naturally and consistently empathetic—these are the people who can easily forge favorable connections with others. They are people who use empathy to engender trust and build bonds; they are catalysts who are able to create positive communities for the greater good." [14] Despite the nature of empathy, Martinuzzi agreed that empathy can be developed and enriched. Stephanie Slamka in her paper, "Humility as a Catalyst for Compassion: The Humility-Compassion Cycle of Helping Relevance to Counseling," discussed how humility, empathy, and wisdom (similar to awareness or knowledge), are all related to compassion and made the following key observations: [15]

- Empathy is comprised of several facets, upon which all humility acts. These facets include a developmental level, reception, reflection, mutuality, and intent for well-being.
- Empathy, humility, and compassion can be cultivated, developed, and improved in various ways.
- Empathy progresses through various steps, just like wisdom, to build on the developmental level of compassion.
- The degrees of humility, empathy, and compassion are different in everyone; each individual is inherently unique in their own context.
- We are born with empathy and humility, and as these concepts are enhanced as the individual develops, it moves in stages of increasing abilities.

BIBLICAL EXAMPLES OF SELF-AWARENESS

There are several examples of self-awareness in the Bible as seen in the lives of Adam, Moses, Joshua, Abraham, Joseph, David, Jesus, Paul, and others. Here are some acts of self-awareness from a few of these leaders:

1. **Adam and Eve**: When Adam and Eve sinned against God, they first became aware of themselves; specifically, that they were naked. Their first response was to try to cover their nakedness for which God asked them, "Who told you were naked? Have you eaten of the fruit of which I commanded you not to" (Genesis 3:7-9). Here we see self-awareness as an intentional effort to discover something new about ourselves or know ourselves better.
2. **David's walk with God**: David's walk with God was so important to him that he was frequently working on his inner self, always being self-aware of his emotions as a way to gain strength and clarity in his walk. David said, "Why are you downcast, O my soul? Why so disturbed within me?" (Psalm 42:5, 11, 43:5). Whatever David was feeling; he wanted it out of his system to walk better with God. We see the importance of self-awareness here when one wants to walk with the Holy Spirit and wants to clear his or her mind positively in the presence of God or of the people he serves. David was self-aware of his sin against God. He said, "For I know my transgressions, and my sin is ever before me. Purge me with hyssop, and I shall be clean; wash me, and I shall be whiter than snow. Create in me a clean heart, O God, and renew a right spirit within me. The sacrifices of God are a broken spirit; a broken and contrite heart, O God, you will not despise" (Psalms 51:3, 7, 10, 17, ESV).
3. **Jesus' examples of self-awareness:** Jesus told his disciples, "If anyone would come after me, let him deny himself and take up his cross and follow me. For whoever would save his life will lose it, but whoever loses his life for my sake will find it" (Matthew 16:24-25). Jesus is calling these leaders to partake in self-denial and to know what is most important in their walk with Him. You can only self-deny what you know you have; you make choices according to the scale of preferences and priorities you know. Jesus is calling leaders to commit to putting Him first above all else and make all sacrifices to put God's agenda above their own. Jesus was self-aware of who was in His encounter with Satan and used that knowledge for victory over all the temptations. His rebuke of Satan, "Away from me, Satan", was an authority based on His

power and identity he knew. When Jesus said to Satan, "You shall not tempt the LORD your God" (Matthew 4:7, NKJV), He was reminding Satan that He was God. He was also self-aware from His declarations that He was the True Vine, the Son of God, the Son of Man, the Living Water, the Light of the World, the Light of Life, the Master, the Friend, the Teacher, the fulfillment of the scriptures, and others, and communicated those to His disciples and others then and now throughout the Gospels.

4. **Teachings from Apostle Paul**: The Apostle Paul said, "Examine yourselves, to see whether you are in the faith. Test yourselves. Or do you not realize this about yourselves, that Jesus Christ is in you?—unless indeed, you fail to meet the test" (2 Corinthians 13:5 ESV). Here, Paul is suggesting we examine ourselves to be aware of ourselves—our faith and the depth of Jesus in us. He also instructed them, saying, "For by the grace given to me, I say to everyone among you not to think of himself more highly than he ought to think, but to think with sober judgment, each according to the measure of faith that God has assigned" (Rom 12.3, ESV). Again, Paul is telling us to think carefully to see ourselves exactly as we are. We need to be self-aware of who we are: "and so, you also must consider yourselves dead to sin and alive to God in Christ Jesus. Let not sin, therefore reign in your mortal body, to make you obey its passions" (Romans 6:11-12).

From the above discussions and scriptural references, Leader-servant's self-awareness can be defined as the self-consciousness of one's personal identity (values, inner strengths, weaknesses, etc.) that foster deep perception and sensitivity in relating to others. We can state that self-awareness is a function of self-examination (self-assessment), inner perceptions, and experiential learning (what experience has taught you about yourself). Self-awareness determines the core qualities of the empathy attribute and is developed through practices that focus on enriching five critical areas:
(1) Self-assessment,
(2) Perception of inner personality,
(3) External perceptions, and
(4) Experiential learning (see Figure 4.2).

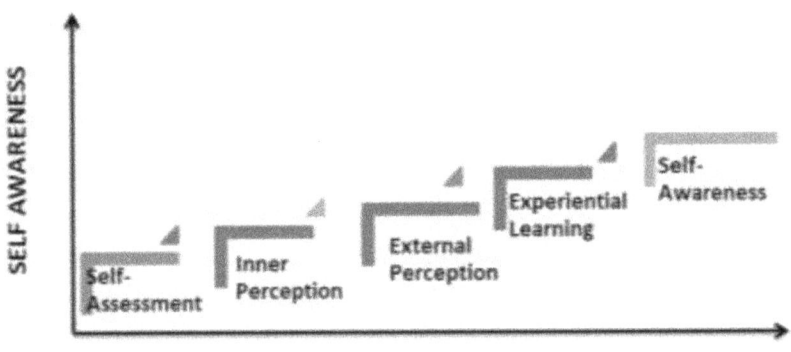

PERSONAL DISCOVERY

Figure 4.2: Self-awareness model: Increasing self-awareness through a three-stage personal discovery process

These practices lead to effective growth in empathy attributes only when they are used. Awareness of your emotions enables you to control negative thoughts better that result from those emotions; one can respond differently and in turn, nurture good relationships. A clear perception of one's thoughts, possible reactions, and behavior patterns is at the core of good and empathetic communication and relationships.

DEVELOP A DESIRE FOR SELF-ASSESSMENTS

Continuous self-assessments require a leader to frequently assess his actions, reactions, and general attitudes toward people in relation to the perception of other people. If the people's perceptions of their leader's behavior toward them are opposite of what the leader feels, there may be something wrong with the way a leader's "good works" is shown or perceived. For example, people feel most valued when they are respected and included; when they feel empowered to engage in high productivity. Such respect and inclusion may be more valued by a worker than the fat raises the leader assumes to be a measure of his or her value of workers. Through self-assessment and by asking tough questions about his or her behavior and getting answers through honest feedback, a leader can test how behaviors should change through an awareness of the areas of focus in his or her development as a leader. A leader-servant must arm him- or herself with this basic character as much as Christ suffered for us in the flesh (1 Peter 4:1). A leader's awareness allows him to perceive the impact of his actions and of people's needs.

With regard to assessing intercultural communication competency and sensitivity skills, one tool that has proven effective is the Intercultural Development Inventory (IDI) developed by Dr. Mitchell Hammer and Dr. Milton Bennett.[16] The IDI instrument assesses a person's Intercultural sensitivity to cultural differences. The authors defined intercultural sensitivity as the ability to recognize multiple perspectives in an event or culture; at the same time, it is also the ability to recognize one's own cultural values and those of others and to develop a positive attitude toward understanding and appreciating cultural differences. Low sensitivity to cultural differences represents a potential obstacle in developing relationships and communicating effectively. A person's intercultural sensitivity can be measured by this index. IDI represents a valid and reliable method to measure individual and group cognitive orientations (worldviews) toward cultural differences. By indicating your current developmental readiness or orientation, IDI guides you or your team in your awareness of developing or advancing intercultural competence and sensitivity. Knowing one's orientation toward cultural differences provides the framework for intercultural competence and a starting point for breaking down barriers to develop relationships and communicate effectively. The IDI profile results provide practical, useful information concerning levels of intercultural competence as identified in the DMIS theory. The other benefits of IDI training include the improvement of a person's cultural compass and suggesting ways one can see and think beyond one's culture; it explains how people or groups tend to think and feel about cultural differences. The IDI provides a structure for understanding how people experience cultural differences and highlight how one's cultural patterns guide and limit one's experience of cultural difference.

DEVELOP AN INNER PERCEPTION OF PERSONALITY

Perception of inner personality refers to having a clear perception of one's personality (strengths, weaknesses, thoughts, beliefs, motivations, and emotions). Correct perception increases a leader's understanding of his- or her character in relation to followers' feelings or difficulties. Knowing your strengths allows you to use that strength to help others; knowing your weaknesses humbles you to identify with the weaknesses of others; knowing your emotions gives you better control when communicating with others. If you are aware that you have problems with anger, you can prepare yourself more effectively to control that anger when dealing with people. If you know that you have the tendency to raise your voice when you speak with people, you can work on controlling your tone of voice when you talk. Perceptions of personality as part of self-awareness are about discovering your inner self and your God-given inner makeup. That allows you to give more of yourself to others without a sense of servitude. This will improve empathy, authenticity, and your relationship with others via t strategies:

Increase the perception of your personality. Self-awareness as an inner dimension of empathy is the perception of one's personality. Self-awareness is the starting point of empathy that allows a person to understand and experience another person's emotional state in a given situation. One must differentiate self-awareness from self-centeredness in which a leader becomes the center and primary focus in all that he or she does.

Gary van Warmerdam, a consultant and trainer in techniques of developing self-awareness as a "Pathway to happiness," referred to self-awareness as "having a clear perception of your personality, including strengths, weaknesses, thoughts, beliefs, motivation, and emotions. It allows you to understand other people, how they perceive you, your attitude, and your responses to them at the moment. "[17] Self-awareness provides the following elements as the starting point in the process of empathy:

- *Clarity to choose* whether you express emotions of love or express emotions out of reactions of fear.
- *Possible moments to catch yourself* prior to saying something destructive or thinking and believing a negative thought.
- *This Means to identifying your unconscious patterns* and raising them in your consciousness, so they can be changed.
- *Pathway to identify the underlying core beliefs* that drive destructive behaviors and create happiness.

Chapter 3
Developing Empathy–Self-Awareness

Understand and use the positive nature of self-awareness. Self-awareness is an innate quality God created in us and it can be used for both the good and the bad. A good example of positive self-awareness can be found in the life of Nelson Mandela, who became the first South African President after 27 years in prison. Attending the inaugural service with many dignitaries, presidents, and world leaders, were three prison guards whom Mandela had personally invited to attend. During his address, President Mandela looked up and asked the three guards to stand up to be recognized. He explained that he personally wanted to recognize and thank them because they treated him with dignity. He also noted that not forgiving those that hurt him during those years would amount to still being in prison. His working them into his speech shows how self-aware forgiveness was part of his healing process. That was empathy. Mandela described it this way:

> "I always knew that, deep down, in every human heart, there are mercy and generosity. Even in the grimmest times in prison, when my comrades and I were pushed to our limits, I would see a glimmer of humanity in one of the guards, perhaps, just for a second, but it was enough to reassure me and keep me going. Man's goodness is a flame that can be hidden but never extinguished." [18]

His self-awareness allowed him to perceive the guards' responsibilities and yet appreciate that their actions were different, especially in the way they treated the prisoners with dignity. Harsher actions might have been justified or had no real negative consequence due to the prevailing political culture.

DEVELOP A SENSE OF EXTERNAL PERCEPTIONS

External perceptions are those outside the inner personality described above. External perceptions include perceptions outside of yourself and perceptions of changes around you and are described below:

Increase perception outside of yourself. The perception outside of you refers to the way a leader is perceived outside of him- or her. The way followers perceive and respond to a leader's ability to improve his self-efficacy (ability to produce the intended result) in a variety of situations can help a leader understand his- or her—strengths and weaknesses—or to be conscious of things previously outside of his or her awareness. A follower's perception of a leader exercising his or her leadership role can also help reveal attitudes of which the leader is not aware. Reactions to, and perceptions of, a leader's normal behavior in pursuing desired results can easily provide a mirror through which a leader can understand him- or herself. Thus, there is a need to pay close attention to how people perceive the leader or even themselves in the company of the leader. For example, people's fear of a leader may reveal a leader that is not kind or pleasant. Understanding followers' lives, what motivates them, what they are sensitive or what makes them feel energized or valued can provide valuable feedback that can improve a leader's self-awareness.

The leader's ability to perceive his environment increases his effectiveness in using teams in decision-making. A team leader must sense and understand the viewpoint of everyone around the table by taking the time and listening to everyone in the group, directing the team in a way that brings everyone together; encouraging people to speak more openly about their frustrations, and raising and handle constructive complaints during meetings. The result is heightened collaboration.

Increase perception of changes around you. Having an awareness of what you want in life reveals what you need to change to achieve a purpose. How you define success in your life determines the path you'll take to get there. It may be that you need to start by refining your definition and attitude toward success. This begins by reexamining perceptions of your thought process; that is, having a clear sense of what you are thinking about and knowing how to best direct it.

Self-awareness through the perception of changes around you assists the leader in identifying areas of his life that need to change to impact the desired change outside. One such area is attitude. Attitude determines a leader's effectiveness, and it is an impact factor in achieving success. As it has been commonly stated, a leader's "attitude will determine his altitude" in leadership. Attitude is formed by habits, and those habits are formed by thoughts. With effective self-awareness, a leader can change his or her thoughts and interpretations, which can also affect emotions positively. One simple change that can be made is in one's relationships with others. Self-awareness of one's emotions can positively affect empathy and therefore, change communication in relationships.

DEVELOP YOURSELF FROM EXPERIENTIAL LEARNING

The common sayings that "experience is the best teacher" and "practice makes perfect" are very fitting practices as pathways for exploring the leader's inner strengths and weaknesses and discovering new solutions in numerous situations, challenges, environments, companies, and expectations. How can CEOs and leaders with several years of experience in a variety of situations deal with life and corporate challenges better than those with limited experience? The "wilderness life experiences" of these leaders have prepared them to understand how to deal with new challenges more effectively. The best leadership training intentionally includes simulations and scenarios of such experiences as coaching strategies. Such training is a way to motivate and encourage people to explore new, unknown roles or situations. Questions and feedback from such training are a very powerful way of helping the leader know him- or herself, gain an accurate self-perception, and develop the ability to analyze an experience for growth and self-awareness.

Let's talk about the wild life experience; how did Jesus Christ, start his ministry and his leadership journey on earth? He first gained some wilderness experience. In Luke 4:1-13, we learn about the "role of wilderness" in a leader's life. Jesus allowed himself to undergo this important experiential learning for 40 days and 40 nights. He was purposeful and determined to go through it. What exactly did he expect to learn about himself in terms of self-awareness? What can we gain from a wilderness experience? Let us consider the following lessons from Luke's account:

Wilderness-need is a source of inner strength to focus on God's provision. In those 40 days, the wilderness provided no food. Jesus intentionally ate nothing but controlled His body. In the end, he was hungry. Knowing His vulnerability for immediate gratification, the devil tempted Him with His immediate and legitimate need to "command this stone to become bread" (Matthew 4:3)) but His answer was "man does not live by bread alone but by every word of God" (Matthew 4:4) In other words, the devil wanted Jesus to use His position and power as the Son of God to meet the need rather than waiting. Jesus was aware of who He was and of the devil's clear devices. Leaders lose focus of who they are or who God is, by focusing on their needs. Wilderness needs can be a source of your inner strength rather than your weakness.

Wilderness-discipline yields dependence on God to keep the mission alive. In His answer to the devil's first temptation, Jesus reminded the devil that the Word of God was an alternative to food and gratification to a leader and had the potential to help the leader grow. He showed that He must depend solely on God for sustenance and to be provided with what was needed. Can you imagine what would have happened to Jesus' ministry and God's purpose if the devil had succeeded in this temptation? The discipline learned from real-life experience provides a leader with full awareness of the source of his strength. Depending on God is most expedient for the mission.

Wilderness power and authority belong only to God. The devil stated, "All this authority I will give you and their glory; for this has been delivered to me and I give to whomever I wish. Therefore, if You will worship before me, all will be Yours" (Matthew 4:8-9, NKJV), James C. Hunt in his book, The Servant, defined power as "the ability to force or coerce someone to do your will, even if they chose not to obey, because of your position or your role and might." [19] We can notice the devil's lie in his statement, claiming the glory and power that belong only to God. How can the devil think he could give Jesus the power he does not have? It is easy to see the content of the devil's temptation: "you will get authority and glory if you worship me." In Jesus' time and even in today's secular world, power and control are important and a desired glory as seen in the self-righteousness of the Pharisees. Devil knew this and saw the opportunity. This is always possible in the wilderness state of suffering. The wilderness walk forces you to either see your vulnerability or how the power of God can be perfect in those vulnerabilities. The choice is yours! We can learn from Jesus' response: He deflected the temptation and showed that power and authority belong only to God and used His authority to command the devil, "Away from me, Satan. You shall worship the Lord thy God and Him only you shall serve" (Matthew 4:10, KJV). A leader seeking power and control, self-promotion, and self-glory cannot be humble and therefore, cannot be an effective leader-servant. However, a leader must be aware of the power he has in service, even in the most daunting circumstances; and uses that power wisely to the glory of God that extended that power to him.

Wilderness battle is won to overcome temptation as part of leadership. The devil tried, even by misquoting the scriptures, to convince Jesus to use His position as the Son of God. In all these experiences, the devil wanted Jesus to prove He was the Son of God to self-promote His power over the power of God. Jesus answered, "You shall not tempt the Lord thy God" (Matthew 4:5, NKJV). Here again, Jesus recognized His authority over the tempter and asserted Himself above the devil. Jesus first led Himself well, to overcome the temptation.

Wilderness suffering is a season of preparation and growth. In the several years of my wilderness journey as a graduate student with a wife, and four children, working full-time on my Ph.D. and financial support only from two part-time jobs to support the family and my education, life was a challenge. We appeared to be "suffering." But was it suffering when it was a choice I made? It was a period of "financial woes" as one of my friends called it. There were periods when we had little food to eat, and some Christmases were celebrated without gifts. And yet, it was a period of utmost stillness in God's presence, a period of increased faith, and, yes, the best period of joy in the Lord. In the "suffering," God provided opportunities for growth. His strength was indeed made more than perfect in my weakness, for I saw nothing in me but that which was focused fully on Him. And, He came through for me! I have always wondered why I was much happier back then than I am now. Yes, the wilderness suffering was a season of preparation and growth.

Wilderness perseverance provides a focused mission. At the end of his wilderness experience, Jesus returned endowed with power and anointing to begin His ministry with focus and few distractions. He had gained a complete sense of self-awareness concerning his mission. The source of our strength, the inner and external battles we must win, and the source of our power as leaders create in us diligent perseverance to focus on finishing whatever God has set before us. Experience is the leader's best teacher in self-leadership.

SUMMARY 3
DEVELOPING EMPATHY–SELF AWARENESS

Before starting this exercise, please read and follow the instruction in the preface of this workbook. Answers to these questions are contained in this chapter. Completion of these exercises after reading the chapter should take 60-90 minutes.

Discovering the Acts of Empathy-Self Awareness

1. The Bible presents us with several example of demonstration of self-awareness in the lives of Adam, Moses, Joshua, Abraham, Joseph, David, Jesus, Paul, and others. Identify the acts of self-awareness of these leaders:
   a. Adam and Eve: (Genesis 3:7-9).
   b. David's walk with God: (Psalm 42:5, 11, 43:5; Psalms 51:3, 7, 10, 17)
   c. Jesus; examples of self-awareness: (Matthew 16:24-25; Matthew 4:7),
   d. Teachings from Apostle Paul: (2 Corinthians 13:5; (Rom 12.3; Romans 6:11-12).
2. How can you define Leader-servant's self-awareness
3. How does Self-awareness determines the core qualities of the empathy attribute
4. What are the key practices of self-a-awareness and
5. How these practices lead to effective growth in empathy attributes only when they are used. Awareness of your emotions

Practicing the Acts of empathy Self-awareness

1. **Empathy-Self-awareness:** Self-awareness as an inner dimension of empathy is the perception of one's personality.
   a. How is self-awareness the starting point of empathy?
   b. How does **self-awareness** contribute to the empathy attribute?
   c. Wilderness suffering is a season of preparation and growth. How can this happen?
2. How does the act of Self-assessments increase self-awareness for empathy
3. How does developing an Inner Perception of Personality increase self-awareness and empathy

4. Self-awareness has been referred as "having a clear perception of your personality, including strengths, weaknesses, thoughts, beliefs, motivation, and emotions. It allows you to understand other people, how they perceive you, your attitude, and your responses to them at the moment. "[32] What roles does self-awareness provides as the starting point in the process of empathy?
5. How can you use the positive nature of self-awareness?
6. What are External Perceptions and how can they increase self-awareness
7. Develop Yourself from Experiential Learning
8. What is the role of "wilderness life experiences" in preparing leaders to deal with challenges more effectively; how did Jesus Christ, start his ministry and his leadership journey on earth? (Luke 4:1-13; Matthew 4:3-1))

CHAPTER 4
DEVELOPING EMPATHY–SYMPATHY

Sympathy is an expression of feeling and concern for others' emotional states based on our perceptions and interpretations of their condition. According to A. J. M. Djiker in *Perceived vulnerability as a common basis of moral emotions*, referred to sympathy as "to be based on the principle of the power to help the vulnerable (young, elderly, and sick) [20] and is usually driven by the instinct to want to care for the person. Clark, Arthur J. Clark in his research paper, *Empathy and Sympathy: Therapeutic Distinctions in Counseling* noted that "Sympathy acts in a way that provides a means of understanding another person's experience or situation, good or bad, with a focus on their well-being." [21] Specific conditions that must occur to experience sympathy include the need for attention to the care receiver, believing that the person needs help and specific characteristics of the given situation that creates the state of need. Without proper undivided attention to the specific situation and need, the care receiver cannot experience sympathy.

There are several biblical situations in which sympathy was expressed. David said, "From the end of the earth I call to You when my heart is faint; Lead me to the rock that is higher than I" (Psalm 61:2, KJV). This is reminding us that God is the rock of salvation and is to be trusted when our heart is sorrowful. Jesus said, "Come unto Me, all who are weary and heavy laden, and I will give you rest" (Matthew 11:28, KJV). This is an expression to reinforce the promises of God's peace in all circumstances. Jesus also gave a very specific message to grievers: "Blessed are those who mourn, for they will be comforted" (Matthew 5:4, KJV). "Do not let your hearts be troubled. Trust in God; trust also in me" (John 14:1). These verses are many like them and are ever-present reminders that God's peace is available to troubled hearts.

These scriptural messages have some key elements in common: they are providing comfort to vulnerable people who may be having some type of challenge in their lives; people who are grieving the loss of someone; or people who are simply yearning for encouragement for various reasons. You can always find these situations in our lives and in the lives of those we lead.

Sympathy consists of the perceptive feelings and concerns that begin the second stage in the process of empathy. These feelings result from self-awareness and are expressed and used effectively through the level of our ability to communicate them. The defining elements for developing sympathy for an effective empathy attribute are sympathetic listening and communication to develop a leader's ability to communicate feelings and concerns in the caregiving relationship. Here are some strategies:

UNDERSTAND EMOTIONS IN COMMUNICATION

Emotions in communication exist in the unspoken words of a conversation. More effective communication leads to better relationships through understanding these emotions. Leaders must focus and understand unspoken (nonverbal) words. Nonverbal words include unspoken words (correctly perceiving unuttered words or feelings); words in the spirit (emotions and feelings expressed through words or experiences); and words hidden in the speaker's spirit (emotions, hurts, joys, etc. that are hidden in the words). This is fully l discussed under Servant Leadership Listening Attribute.

SUMMARY 4
DEVELOPING EMPATHY–SYMPATHY

Before starting this exercise, please read and follow the instruction in the preface of this workbook. Answers to these questions are contained in this chapter. Completion of these exercises after reading the chapter should take 60-90 minutes.

Discovering the Acts of Empathy-Sympathy

1. "Sympathy acts in a way that provides a means of understanding another person's experience or situation, good or bad, with a focus

on their well-being." [21] what are the specific conditions that must occur to experience sympathy
2. How was sympathy expressed in the following bibilical examples:
   a. David (Psalm 61:2, KJV).
   b. Jesus (Matthew 11:28, KJV). (Matthew 5:4, KJV). (John 14:1).
3. What are the defining elements for developing sympathy for an effective empathy attribute? What are some strategies to develop those:

Practicing the Acts of Empathy-sympathy

1. **Empathy-Sympathy** - an expression of feeling and concern for others' emotional states based on our perception and interpretation of that state.
   a. What are the specific conditions that must occur to experience sympathy?
   b. How do you develop empathy-compassion?
   c. How do you practice humility to maximize Empathy and Compassion; or Emulate the Empathy of a leader?
2. How can a leader develop a sense of Personal Empathy?
3. Identify five key elements of complete compassionate empathy.

CHAPTER 5
DEVELOPING EMOTIONAL SELF-REGULATION

Emotional self-regulation is the capacity to regulate and control one's emotions to channel attention for the good of another person. This is the stage above just feelings and concerns. It involves controlling the emotions that allow you to enter and walk through that person's emotional state by applying the deeper perspective of the care receiver's experiences. Broadened experiences of the caregiver usually help in regulating one's emotions effectively. Psychologists generally agree that "emotions are specific and intense psychological and physical reactions to a particular **event.** These emotions can be the result or reaction to an event or experience, subjective individual expression of feelings, physiological response (fight-or-flight reaction), or expressive behavioral actions such as facial expression, tone of voice, restlessness, or other body languages. [22] Our primary emotions that need regulating include feelings such as joy, fear, love, hatred, sadness, surprise, and anger. Sympathy, self-awareness, and compassion are all critical elements that complete empathy in Servant leadership. Without the capacity to control and channel one's emotion to the benefit of the other person; however, empathy will not bring the needed healing to others.

Self-regulation means having a good understanding and control of how one can relate to others and an ability to adjust one's behavior to relate positively to people or manage others' emotions and weaknesses. You can only change a behavior that you know! A leader who has an understanding of what can anger him or her will have the ability to improve self-control as an important part of disciplining the body. Jesus' self-awareness of his mission and how significant the mission was to the Father dictated all his actions and responses to issues. Our awareness (not ignorance) of the devices of the enemy equips us to handle the devil's subtleties better, intended to draw us into ungodliness. Increased emotional capacity is required to lead people effectively in the presence of difficulties and can be developed through the following strategies:

Express and channel your emotions directly to God. As found in the Scriptures, David and Paul, for example, know how to express and channel their emotions directly to God, gaining empathy and comfort from the Lord. David expressed his different feelings and usually found comfort and empathy from God's promises. He said, "And why should you moan over me and be disquieted within me? Hope in God and wait expectantly for Him, for I shall yet praise Him, my Help and my God" (Psalm 42:5, NKJV). These scriptures also suggest ways to control these emotions, including putting our hope in God, prayer, and supplications.

Be sensitive to and considerate of others' feelings. A careful understanding of others' feelings and including those feelings expressed in decision-making increases people's security and confidence in articulating their feelings and therefore, in helping a leader improve his empathy attribute. There may be introverted people in the organization who by nature are people of few words or extroverted people; with too many words and energy to express themselves. These two personality traits express feelings differently, and intentional effort must be made to be sensitive to their different responses. Some people are encouraged to express more of their feelings by a leader showing that he or she is paying attention through such gestures as nodding, smiling, or looking at them directly in affirmation.

Know the correct perceptions of yourself to increase your emotional capacity. Having a clear perception of yourself means that you can better control your life as it affects those you serve and your ability to choose the appropriate response for a given situation. A sense of how one perceives him- or herself is at the core of one's quality of life. How one perceives him- or herself often determines self-esteem, self-confidence, and attitudes in several aspects of life. If you perceive yourself as a child of God, your attitude will reflect the values of a child of God; if you perceive yourself as a leader-servant, you will adopt key behaviors that reflect humility and servant-hood; if you perceive yourself as a failure, you will always and quickly act as a failure. A failed attempt in a venture does not make one a failure. A sense of failure is a false sense of perception; if you perceive yourself as an achiever, you will work to develop the attitude of an achiever. These are simple facts of life!

A correct perception of yourself increases your self-leadership and ability to lead others because perception as an element of self-awareness allows you to identify things you want to change and improve. In self-leadership, you are the only person who has the power to influence change in yourself. We have discussed the importance of value systems (faith, preference, self-control, love, beliefs, etc.). By having a correct perception of how we come across when we communicate with others about our feelings and attitudes, we can enter and walk through someone's experiences and bring them appropriate healing without adding to their hurt.

SUMMARY 5
DEVELOPING EMOTIONAL SELF-REGULATION

Before starting this exercise, please read and follow the instruction in the preface of this workbook. Answers to these questions are contained in this chapter. Completion of these exercises after reading the chapter should take 60-90 minutes

Discovering the Acts of Emotional Self-regulation

1. What does self-regulation mean? What is emotional self-regulation?
2. What is involved in your emotional self-regulation?
3. What are your primary emotions that need regulating?
4. Increased emotional capacity is required to lead people effectively in the presence of difficulties. What are strategies that you can develop
5. How do you express and channel your emotions directly to God; see David (Psalm 42:5)

Practicing the Acts of Emotional self-regulation

1. When was the last time you lost control, maybe out of anger or some other unresolved issues? What was the outcome of your desired purpose?
2. Why is the capacity to control and channel one's emotion to the benefit of the other person important in leadership?
3. Why is self-awareness an important starting point in in practicing self-regulation? How did Jesus demonstrate the quality of self-awareness in his mission
4. What strategies will you adopts to increase you emotional capacity to lead people effectively in the presence of difficulties.

CHAPTER 6
DEVELOPING EMPATHY– COMPASSION

Servant leadership is about serving and caring for others. It takes self-awareness, the ability to perceive feelings, and expressing concern to responsively meet verbalized needs through compassion. The leader-servant extends himself to help ease pain actively and is not contented with just the feeling or showing concern. It is the last stage that puts all the first acts to affect the desired wellness of a person through empathy. Key elements of compassion for servant leadership attributes can be summarized below:

- Compassion is generally referred to as *sharing in someone's suffering* together with that person.
- Compassion is more broadly known as the *emotional response of sharing* in the suffering of another person along with an *intentional desire to alleviate or reduce the suffering* to make that person whole.
- Compassion can also be referred to as *hearing and understanding another's suffering* and having the wisdom to know how to alleviate that suffering.
- Compassion is an *element of empathy* and is often differentiated from the other elements of empathy by the intentional actions a person with compassion performs to aid the person to whom he feels sympathetic.
- Compassion involves *intentionally engaging the spiritual aspect of empathy* to help the care-receiver find healing, rest, and affirmation in God.
- Compassion involves *deeper engagement in the process of walking* through the valley of a situation through broadened experience and emulating God's empathy.
- Compassion occurs when there is an *intentional act to alleviate the suffering* of another person more than just emotions and sympathy.

From the above elements, compassionate empathy is the act of compassion given beyond just sympathy to bring wellness to a person. A leader walks along with someone in that individual's "wilderness" state of suffering or danger through these four stages of empathy. However, only with compassion, motivated by selfless love, will empathy result in a greater effect on the wellness of a person. Here are some strategies to help us develop compassionate empathy:

DEVELOP A HEART OF HUMILITY

As we humble ourselves before others, we can care for them more as an example of being Christ-like. We must learn to naturally practice humility to maximize empathy and compassion. Following the model developed by Slamka [15] based on the idea of humility as a catalyst of empathy and constant assistant to compassion, as an individual develops in personal leadership, so do empathy and compassion at differing levels. Acts of humility at each level of developing empathy build the foundation for compassion and help us be more other-centered in service leadership. At this stage of awareness, we can see ourselves at the equal human level, though different callings. Consider the following model scenario:

Practice Model

Practice 1: Imagine Person A is walking down the street. She is humble and therefore, is open to seeing others in her reality. Her humility allows her to see people on the human level she occupies; no one is greater or lesser than she is.

Practice 2: Person B, who is also carrying the capacity of humility, crosses paths with Person A and sees Person A as just a human possessing the same qualities. They mutually and equally recognize one another. Neither shares any desire to become superior or powerful over the other; neither wishes to become submissive. They just accept each other as they are—humbly equal.

Practice 3: Imagine now that Person B is in a state of suffering. Person A, seeing Person B suffering, still recognizes and judges both as equal despite Person B's state. How do they hear each other and share their suffering together? Here's an example:

Person A sees Person B as the same and can reflect her suffering with the attitude of "We are identical, humans that can feel pain the same way." Person A says, "Friend, how are you feeling, are you OK?"

He says this with an inclined expression of concern and an open caring body posture. (This signals recognition and awareness).

Person B answers, "I am not sure, anxious and looking worried; I just cannot find my purse and am running late to work"

Person A follows with a deeper reflection of suffering, "I see you are upset," with the intent of assisting in Person B's well-being. Person A then says, "Let me make sure I am hearing you correctly. You are saying you are upset because you missed the bus and are running late for work?" (This is an empathetic reflection to show understanding and care).

After Person B responds in the affirmative, Person 'A' offers to help: "I understand. Can I help you by driving you to work?" (Exhibiting compassion and suffering shared).

The greater the degree of humility, the stronger it acts to build and sustain empathy and the more advanced a leader becomes in expressing empathy in service to others. In the above example, humility listening translates into empathetic listening to express "Your suffering means something to me, because we are the same. I do not wish to feel pain nor do I wish to be different than you." Alternatively, it can translate to "Let me help ease your suffering so that we are the same again and are both at peace." The very nature of humility is to provide an open door for well-being, which is at the core of empathy and compassion. When someone is unpretentious, like Person A, he or she does not feel the need to be superior to another person; Person B in suffering is also humble and does not feel inferior. They do not engage in power struggles during interpersonal experiences; they do not need to have the last word, and so on. A person who is feeling humble thinks to bring the two to the same level so they can be on equal footing. This could mean adapting to meet the requirements of the other's culture.

EMPATHY-COMPASSION IS SHARING AND CARING

A call for compassion is a call to bless someone by sharing and caring for that person. The Apostle Peter exhorts Christians, individually and collectively, to have compassion for one another in humility and tenderness of heart: "Finally, all *of you be* of one mind, having compassion for one another; love as brothers, *be* tenderhearted, *and be* courteous". (1 Peter 3:8). Apostle Paul has a similar message and call for compassion through sharing and caring for one another without division: "The members should have the same care for one another. And if one member suffers, all the members suffer with it; or if one member is honored, all the members rejoice with it (1 Corinthians 12:25-26, NJKV). In his example, to the weak, he became as weak to win the weak and became "all things to all men" that he "might, by all means, save some." Paul "by all means" implies that we must make intentional efforts to give a helping hand to a follower in need. This is walking through someone else's experience to bring wholeness. Paul became all things to all men without compromising his values. To the Ephesians believers, Paul also wrote that all must "be kind to one another, tenderhearted, forgiving one another, even as God in Christ forgave you". (Ephesians 4:32). These leaders, including the Apostle James, demonstrated that a call to compassion is an intentional and practical response to walk-in service in the suffering of the most vulnerable of God's children; including widows, widowers, and orphans. "Pure and undefiled religion before God and the Father is this: to visit orphans and widows in their trouble and to keep oneself unspotted from the world." (James 1:27, NKJV).

EMULATE THE EMPATHY OF GOD

Jesus in the human form experienced human temptation and was, therefore, able to empathize with human experiences. He became a human chief advocate in the presence of God: "For we do not have a High Priest who cannot sympathize with our weaknesses, but was in all points tempted as we are, yet without sin. Let us, therefore, come boldly to the throne of grace, that we may obtain mercy and find grace to help in time of need" (Hebrews 4:15-16, NKJV). This presents Jesus as our compassionate High Priest to model our lives after. Through Jesus, then, God is revealed as one with both the capacity to know human experiences and He has the power and commitment to actively do so. In several miracles Jesus performed and the temptations he endured, he identified with the human experience, battling the diseases and afflictions of others, pain, suffering, and death (2 Corinthians 5:21).

CHAPTER 6
DEVELOPING EMPATHY–COMPASSION

Leo Babuata, who posted on his blog "Guide to Cultivating Compassion in Your Life, With 7 Practices," argued that the key to developing compassion in one's life is to make it a daily practice.[23] In the same light, consider the following four strategies for developing relational empathy:

1. **Imagine experiencing the other's suffering.** Imagine that a loved one is suffering. Something terrible has happened to him or her. Now try to imagine the pain the person is experiencing. Imagine the suffering in as much detail as possible. This means that you should experience the other person's suffering or emotions from that person's frame of reference as if you are in that person's shoes. Jesus, in observing the widow who lost her only son and was going to bury him, sensed the woman's pain and approached the funeral procession, and resurrected her son. "And when the Lord saw her, he had compassion on her and said to her, 'Do not weep.' Then he came up and touched the bier, and the bearers stood still. And he said, 'Young man, I say to you, arise'" (Luke 7:11-16, NIV).

2. **Practice the act of kindness.** Imagine that you are Person B in Practice 2 (from the Practice Model above), and are suffering. Now imagine that another human being would like your suffering to end. What would you like that person to do to end your suffering? Now reverse roles: you are the person who desires for the other person's suffering to end. What would you do to help ease the suffering or end it completely? Practice doing something each day to help end the suffering of others, even in a tiny way. The door of a leader's heart for love and kindness is opened to the level of his empathy attribute. It allows us to be better aware of the need to ease someone else's pain. *"Rejoice with those who rejoice, weep with those who weep"* (Romans 12:15).

3. **Practice relieving others' suffering.** Imagine the suffering of a human being you've met recently. Reflect on how happy or relieved that person would feel if you can, act to help that person. That's the feeling you want to develop. With constant practice, that feeling can be grown and nurtured. A study by the Forbes group suggests that the more you meditate on compassion, the more your brain reorganizes itself to feel empathy toward others.[24] "But whoever has this world's goods, and sees his brother in need, and

shuts up his heart from him, how does the love of God abide in him?" (1 John 3:17). This is a direct command to leaders to love and care for our neighbor (Matthew 22:39; 1 Peter 4:8).

4. **Take a personal interest in people.** Showing people by real action not feeling that you care about them is one way to share in their experiences and their lives. These experiences can be explored further through intentional efforts to get to know people, asking questions about their daily activities, personal lives, hobbies, challenges, and families more so than just feelings about work. Show that you value people as people first before your value them as employees. One can show personal interest in people by being authentic and recognizing and affirming people with genuine praise and making oneself approachable. Effective empathetic leaders pay attention to what people are doing, not to punish or micro-manage them, but for the primary purpose of affirming them with specific praise for those things or sharing in their challenges. When you give praise or share in the struggles, make your genuine words memorable: "I share your pain in the loss of your _____; you can take some time off to get some relief." Compassion occurs when you're not only recognizing the pain but making some sacrifice to relieve the pain.

A CASE OF COMPLETE EMPATHY

A case of complete empathy demonstrates the act of self-awareness to empathy-compassion. Recall the definition of personal empathy as the inner strength quality of a leader-servant that affords the required sympathy, compassion, and responsiveness to care for the follower in a way that builds that person up in that experience. Such personal empathy leads to compassion through direct intimate involvement in alleviating suffering. The accounts of the feeding of four thousand and the Parable of the Good Samaritan clearly illustrate the kind of complete sympathy, self-regulation, and compassion in the process of personal and spiritual empathy toward others. Jesus said:

> *A man was going down from Jerusalem to Jericho, and he fell among robbers, who stripped him and beat him and departed, leaving him half*

dead. But a Samaritan, as he journeyed, came to where he was, and when he saw him, he had compassion. He went to him and bound up his wounds, pouring on oil and wine. Then he set him on his own animal and brought him to an inn and took care of him. And the next day he took out two denarii and gave them to the innkeeper, saying, 'Take care of him, and whatever more you spend, I will repay you when I come back.' (Luke 10:32-35, ESV).

We can identify five key elements of complete compassionate empathy in this Parable:

- **Empathic Connection to** an emotional experience or situation. The man was beaten and was hurting in a poor emotional state; he was a "sheep" in a state of suffering and needed help.
- **Empathetic awareness**. The Samaritan looked and saw him; when he saw him, he understood a person in such a state needed help (awareness); he was aware and fully engaged to help.
- **Empathetic sympathy**. The Samaritan showed concern and feelings of pity toward him because he came to where he was (sympathy). Indeed, the Samaritan cared and shared his feelings...
- **Empathetic regulation**. The Samaritan took intentional steps to control his emotions and instead focused on how this man must have been beaten to point of death. His self-regulation allowed him to be calm enough to think. He controlled any element of fear for his safety.
- **Empathetic compassion**. He reached full compassion: he took direct and personal steps and *"went to him and bound up his wounds, pouring on oil and wine"* (Luke 10:34, ESV). He walked into the experience to meet the man's immediate needs; he was shocked, obviously, but proceeded first to control the man's immediate emotion of pain, feeling the pressure as he got fully involved in the experience. He shared the suffering of the man by relinquishing the right of his time, donkey, and money and brought him to an inn, where he committed to additional care. This is a pure illustration of loving humanity and an example of Leader-Servant leadership.

The critical element of compassion is that it must lead to personal action to ease the state of suffering of another person. According to Pastor Lance Lecocq of Monroeville Assembly of God, "The heart of compassion is to consider the needy, be personally involved in caring for them with whatever we have, and have a positive 'sheep-itude' toward them, which he defined as caring attitude for the sheep. We need to look for opportunities for the sheep to experience God's love."

In the Bible story of the feeding of four thousand (Matthew 15:30-35) we find the same elements fully illustrated; the emotional experience of a multitude that was weary and hungry, and Jesus' awareness of the situation: "I have compassion for these people. They have already been with me three days and have nothing to eat. I do not want to send them away hungry, or they may collapse on the way" (Matthew 15: 33, NIV) Jesus' expression of concern and feeling toward them, (sympathy) and willing to provide for them with both his emotional control of the situation and his intentional steps (compassion) to ease their pain with food and comfort: "They all ate and were satisfied" (Matthew 15:37, NIV).

These exemplify the elements of empathy in servant leadership. These words mean that Jesus' ultimate goal was to heal the people's spiritual weariness and, in an act of compassion, He took personal steps to accomplish that. He saw the followers were not only weary but scattered, lost, helpless, and without a shepherd to guide them. The awareness of these elements drove His emotional feeling to the highest level of compassion.

SELF-CENTEREDNESS PARALYZES COMPASSION

In contrast to the above examples, the story of the rich young ruler illustrates a case where compassion was lacking. The young ruler, who was desirous of eternal life, came to Jesus passionately seeking to know the truth concerning eternal life and how he could obtain it. He said, "'Honor your father and your mother,' and 'You shall love your neighbor as yourself.' ... go, sell what you have and give to the poor, and you will have treasure in heaven; and come, follow Me". (Matthew 19:16-21, NKJV). The young ruler lacked compassion because he loved himself more than others and could not walk alongside another person in a state of suffering or poverty. Several important lessons can be derived from this negative example of empathy, which reflects self-centeredness:

- **Improper perception and self-awareness.** The young, rich ruler could not see how he could love his neighbor more than his material possessions. Furthermore, he did not have a correct understanding of who Jesus was; he thought that by doing the "good thing" and keeping the commandments, he could inherit internal life. Hence, he had no pity or emotions, or feelings for the poor.
- **Lack of Commitment to Love.** The young ruler failed to understand the full meaning of the commandment "You shall love your neighbor as yourself" (Matthew 19:19, NIV). This is where he completely lost any sense of empathetic compassion and showed interest in personal involvement with no one other than himself.
- **Self-centeredness and blindness.** The young man had an incorrect perception of what was most important. He knew that he had many possessions and was unwilling to sacrifice the temporary things for the eternal things he was seeking. However, his self-awareness of his position and wealth resulted in selfishness and self-centeredness and blinded him from seeing a better future. What a tragedy!
- **Tightfisted and Proud.** He was sad primarily because he could not part with his possessions to extend love to others. "He went away sorrowful, for he had great possessions" (Matthew 19:22, NKJV). It was important to Jesus for the rich young ruler to deal with his love for his possessions before he could correctly perceive the real meaning of Jesus' mission to follow him.

To answer our beginning question, what motivates a leader to *empathize* with a follower, we could see that love-motivated selfless compassion is the ultimate driver for empathy. A leader trapped in self-centeredness is often unwilling to give up positional rights to show real compassion for others. Lack of compassion is borne out of the lack of humility, the lack of a commitment to love others, and the unwillingness to take personal responsibility for the well-being of others. Can you imagine yourself or anyone else exhibiting these four qualities? At what level will you begin to develop the correct attitude of compassion? This young ruler from the first level—a much-needed level of self-awareness for others' needs. Without an intentional effort to understand people's state of needs, you cannot build any feelings or emotions toward the situation.

A Case of Sharing Self in Empathy

One experience comes to mind that demonstrates these points. It was a rainy evening in New Orleans when we received a call from a couple of friends of ours of several years. We will call our Brother Dr. X, an engineer with a reputable firm, and his wife, Sister Y, a nurse. Both are seasoned and respected children of God, married for more than fifteen years, and doing well financially.

At the other end of the line was a frantic plea from Sister Y: "Bro Wosu, your Brother Mr. X and I are through; I cannot handle this anymore. I have packed my stuff and I am ready to go with my children and never return to this marriage."

As my wife and I wondered what could have gone wrong with this loving couple, we reflected on their wonderful relationship, their work in the faith, and their four beautiful children.

The time was 9:15 PM and the couple lived three hours away. My wife and I immediately gathered a few changes of clothing and jumped into our car and headed to meet the couple. About 30 minutes from their house, our old sport Jaguar stalled in the middle of the road at a traffic light under the heavy rain storm. For the next several minutes, with no umbrella or raincoat, I tried to figure out what was wrong with a car that had no problems before tonight. We did not really know what to do but pray. After a few minutes of prayers, miraculously, as if the car heard our rebuke, the car started without any real intervention except shaking the battery cable. One wonders why this car stopped in the middle of the road after two hours of highway driving and stopped at the first traffic light as we exited toward their house. We leave that for the Lord; however, we arrived at our friends' home just before 12:45 AM.

The brethren were waiting; they were now weary and tired from several hours or maybe days or weeks of quarrels. This couple we knew as friends, now looked so down that the joy that usually defined them was not there; it was replaced with hurt and sorrow.

There was no time for pleasantries. We immediately changed our wet clothes and sat down to talk. The couple, especially the husband Dr. X, who is naturally the quiet type, was not ready to talk. For the next four hours, there was neither understanding nor agreement to even one disagreement. The tension was too high, and both were determined that their marriage was over.

Chapter 6
Developing Empathy–Compassion

At about 3:45 AM, I called a time-out for everyone to have a quiet moment to pray or rest for 15 minutes. We resumed a few minutes later. At this time, I felt the Lord prompting my spirit to change the approach. My wife and I now started sharing our personal experiences on the specific issues with which they were battling. We validated their different hurts and shared the responsibilities in their conflicts; we tried to separate the major issues from the minor issues and shared how we had worked together to resolve similar issues effectively. We were shamelessly transparent and honest in the sharing. We shared with them how what they see as a major issue was really the accumulation of unresolved issues over several years, and that no one really wins in the conflict but the devil himself whose major goal is, to destroy their partnership. We related the enemy's plan to destroy or impede the work of God to our car experience. We got some laughs over that, for the first time. There was a breakthrough. We all walked through the same experience with the car to see that it was the devil that was at work. He had tried to stop us in the middle of the road to block us from reaching them. By relating the encounter with the car, they could see in reality how the devil can be at work to destroy the children of God, even marriages. Could this be why God allowed this car experience? I am not sure. What followed convinced me that the empathy we are talking about could be an effective way to bring healing to hurting souls.

Now the time was 5:15 AM when our brother Dr. X, who before this time was mostly closed to any suggestions for agreement, began to open up and ask questions. There were some tears. We saw healing beginning to occur, apologies began to be rendered and accepted. They shared with us how they had gone through several rounds of counseling in two states on these issues, but nothing had impacted them more than the experiences we had shared and our ability to understand and walk beside them. They were humbled knowing that we too had gone through such experiences. That empathy produced a change in them and led to their willingness to allow healing. Today, this couple remains best of friends to one another and still cannot believe that what happened actually happened.

Summary 6
Developing Empathy–Compassion

Before starting this exercise, please read and follow the instruction in the preface of this workbook. Answers to these questions are contained in this chapter. Completion of these exercises after reading the chapter should take 60-90 minutes.

Discovering the Acts of Empathy-Compassion

1. Why and how is compassion the highest level of the empathy act?
2. The leader-servant extends himself to help ease pain actively and is not contented with just the feeling or showing concern. What is compassionate empathy? What are the key elements of compassion for servant leadership attributes?
3. Developing a heart of humility is one strategy to help us develop compassionate empathy. Based on the idea of humility as a catalyst of empathy and constant assistant to compassion, how does an act of humility build the foundation for compassion for empathy?
4. A call for compassion is a call for intentional and practical response to walk-in service in the suffering of others and to bless someone by sharing and caring for that person. How did The Apostle Peter demonstrate this concepts (1 Peter 3:8) and. Apostle Paul (1 Corinthians 12:25-26, NJKV). (Ephesians 4:32). (James 1:27, NKJV).
5. Jesus in the human form experienced human temptation and was, therefore, able to empathize with human experiences. What are His four strategies for developing relational empathy:
    a. Luke 7:11-16.
    b. Romans 12:15.
    c. (1 John 3:17; Matthew 22:39; 1 Peter 4:8).

Practicing the Acts of Empathy-Compassion

1. Personal empathy leads to compassion through direct intimate involvement in alleviating suffering illustrated in the feeding of four thousand and the Parable of the Good Samaritan (Luke 10:32-35, ESV). What are the five key elements of complete compassion-empathy in these accounts in the Parables:

CHAPTER 6
DEVELOPING EMPATHY–COMPASSION

2. The critical element of compassion is that it must lead to personal action to ease the state of suffering of another person.
    a. How does Self-Centeredness Paralyze Compassion (Matthew 19:16-21, NKJV)?
    b. What motivates a leader to *empathize* with a follower?

3. How can practical care or service rendered in serving others be an act of compassion?)

Topic Index

About This Book, 22
Affective Compassion, 77
authentic, 24, 26, 86
authentic leadership, 37
Authentic Leadership, 45
Authenticity, 43
Comfort, 41
commitment, 19, 25, 60, 84, 89
communication
   types of, 30
Communication, 30
Comparisons
   with other works, 40
Compassion, 28, 53, 54, 55, 59, 83, 85, 87
   definition, 81
compassionate relational empathy, 75
Continuous self-assessments, 62
credibility, 48
critical element of compassion, 87, 93
Cultivating Compassion
   Practice empathy, 85
   Practice relief of suffering, 85
   Practice the act of kindness, 85
   Take a personal interest in people, 86
cultural differences, 63
Daniel Goleman, 51
David, 60
dependence on God, 57, 68
emotional capacity, 77, 78, 79
Empathetic regulation, 87
empathy
   related to compassion, 59
   the experience or self-awareness, 52
Empathy, 54, 56, 73
   Empathy-compassion, 53
   Empathy-Sympathy, 52

Empathy of God, 84
Empathy-attribute, 28, 54, 56
EMPATHY-COMPASSION, 75
EMPATHY-SYMPATHY, 75
Emulate, 75, 84
Experiential Learning, 67, 71
focus, 57
Functional Definitions, 35
giving, 74
humility, 54, 59, 83, 89
Humility –listening, 83
Initiative
   definition of, 29
inside-out, 46
Joshua, 19
lack of compassion, 88
Lack of Compassion
   Improper perception, 89
   Lack of Commitment, 89
   Self-centeredness and blindness, 89
   Tightfisted and Proud, 89
law of, 42
LEADER, 28, 52
Leader as Servant Leadership, 42
   definition, 25
Leader First., 23
Leader-as-Servant Leadership, 23
leader-servant's affection-attribute
   definition, 48
leadership, 25
Leadership Attributes, 43
Leadership Inner Value system, 25
Model, 23
Moses, 19
Navigation-attribute, 48
Pastor Lance Lecocq, 87
Perception
   of Changes to make, 66
   outside of self, 65, 71
Perception of Inner Personality

of Inner Personality, 63
of Inner Personality, 63
of Inner Personality, 70
PERCEPTION OF PERSONALITY
   in Self awareness, 62, 70
Personal Outward Authenticity, 47
Power, 68, 69
Practicing Servant Leadership Empathy, 57
process, 25
relationships, 74
self-awareness, 51, 61, 65, 69, 70, 77, 79, 89
Self-awareness, 54, 61, 70
   create innate quality by God, 65, 71
   definition of, 64, 70
   identifies areas of life that need change, 66
Sense, 75, 86
Servant, 23, 24
sheep-itude, 88
Stephanie Slamka, 59
suffering, 53, 54, 57, 69, 70, 85, 86, 87, 92
Sympathy, 52, 54, 73, 87
   definition, 73

perception of feelings, 74
Teachable Moments to Grow, 79
test
   for leader-servant authenticity, 46
   of essential elements of personal authenticity, 46, 47
The Leadership Influence-attribute, 41
The Principle of Leadership Empathy-Attribute, 28, 55
The Principle of Leadership Adaptability Attribute, 27
The Principle of Leadership listening-attribute, 30
Understanding
   of Emotions in Communications, 74
weaknesses, 61, 63, 64, 66, 71, 77
Wilderness
   battle, 69
   Discipline, 57, 68
   Need, 67
   Perseverance, 69
   Power, 68
   Suffering, 69, 70
wilderness experience, 67

REFERENCES

[1]Greenleaf, R. (1970). *The Servant as Leader,* Indianapolis: The Robert K. Greenleaf Center

[2]Spears, L. (1996*).* *"Reflections on Robert K. Greenleaf and servant-leadership."* Leadership & Organization Development Journal, 17(7), 33-35

[3]Russell, R.F. (2001). "The role of values in servant leadership." *Leadership & Organization Development Journal,* 22(2), 76-83

[4]Russell, R.F., and Stone, A.G. (2002). "A review of servant leadership attributes: developing a practical model." *Leadership & Organization Development Journal,* 23(3), 145-15

[5]Terry. R. W (1993*). Authentic Leadership: Courage In Action*, San Francisco, CA, Jossey-Bass

[6]George, B (2003). *Authentic Leadership: Rediscovering the Secrets to Creating Lasting Value.* San Francisco, CA, Jossey-Bass

[7]Shamir, B. & Eilam, G. (2005). "What's your story? Toward a life-story approach to authentic leadership." Leadership Quarterly, 16, 395–418.

[8]Anderson, GL (2009). *Advocacy Leadership: Toward a Post-Reform Agenda in Education,* Routledge, New York, 41

[9]Yacobi, B.G. *"Elements of Human Authenticity."* http://www.philosophytogo.org /wordpress/?p=1945, Retrieved, July 15, 2012

[10]George, B (2003). *Authentic Leadership: Rediscovering the Secrets to Creating Lasting Value,* San Francisco, CA, Jossey-Bass

[11]Wosu, SN (2014), *Leader as Servant Leadership Model,* Xulon Press

[12]Daniel Coleman (1997). *Emotional Intelligence.* New York: Bantam Books, 1997. Read more: http://www.humanillnesses.com/Behavioral-Health-Br-Fe/Emotions.html#ixzz2MpKlR6V0

[13]http://en.wikipedia.org/wiki/Sympathy

[14] Martinuzzi, Bruna (2009) "The Leader as a Mensch: Become the Kind of Person Others Want to Follow," Six Seconds

[15] Slamka, S (2010). "Humility as a Catalyst for Compassion The Humility-Compassion Cycle of Helping Relevance to Counseling", College of St. Joseph In Vermont http://compassionspace.com/sg_userfiles/revised_humility-compassion.pdf

[16] Hammer, M. R., Bennett, M. J., & Wiseman, R. (2003). "Measuring intercultural sensitivity: The Intercultural Development Inventory." In R. M. Paige (Guest Ed.). Special issue on the Intercultural Development. International Journal of Intercultural Relations, 27(4), 421–443.

[17] Warmerdam. GV. Self-Awareness: Pathway to Happiness, http://www.pathwaytohappiness.com/self-awareness.htm , Retrieved July 10, 2013

[18] Nelson Mandela (1994), Long walk to Freedom, Little, Brown and Company, New York.

[19] Hunt, J. C (1998). The Servant. Prima Publishing Roseville, CA, p. 30.

[20] Djiker, A. J. M. (2010). "Perceived vulnerability as a common basis of moral emotions". British Journal of Social Psychology 49: 415–423.

[21] Clark, Arthur J. (2010). "Empathy and Sympathy: Therapeutic Distinctions in Counseling". Journal of Mental Health Counseling 32 (2): 95–101.

[22] http://www.humanillnesses.com/Behavioral-Health-Br-Fe/Emotions.html.

[23] http://zenhabits.net/a-guide-to-cultivating-compassion-in-your-life-with-7-practices/

[24] http://www.forbes.com/feeds/hscout/2008/03/27/hscout613899.html

www.ingramcontent.com/pod-product-compliance
Lightning Source LLC
LaVergne TN
LVHW050024080526
838202LV00069B/6911